Key Quest

The Inner Journey of the Entrepreneur

Commitment to Purpose
The Spirit of Helping Others
The Practice of Meditation

Tony Rubbo

Key Quest © Anthony M. Rubbo, Sr. 2022
ISBN: 9798885670418
Key Quest, related to this book, is published by,
and is a trademark of Anthony M. Rubbo, Sr. 2022

The Keyholder (song lyrics) © Anthony M. Rubbo, Sr. 2012

The following are trademarks of Anthony M. Rubbo, Sr. 2022, referring to games and game activities: *The Hero's Journey, 21 GEMs, The Eternal Clock, Key Quotes, The Year of the Entrepreneur, Master Key, Keys* to Adventure, *Time Portal, PIE Chart, The Inner Marathon, M-NON (aka Emanon), Search for Hidden Treasure (aka Roll & Scroll), The Key Quest Entrepreneurial Spirit Awards, The Key Quest Awards.*

All rights reserved.
Please contact Tony Rubbo for special rights for use.

Website: tonyrubbo.com
Email: tonyrubbo133@gmail.com

The Front Cover

The front cover image represents the 'Golden Ratio'.

Following the movement of the squares
and the curves within the squares,
the image moves infinitely inward.

This symbolizes the Key Quest principle
of moving toward one's innermost nature,
to assure experiencing inner peace
while achieving outer success.

See page 234 for a Key Quest Insight regarding the 'Golden Ratio'.

Internet search *the Golden Ratio* or *the Fibonacci Sequence* for more.

The Key Theme

The word 'key' appears throughout this book. As an adjective,
it can mean important, central, significant, higher, inner.

As a noun, it refers to the idea of something that can
open the doors to positive outcomes, experiences, etc.

For example, *commitment to one's purpose* is a key that can
open the doors to peace and to personally responsible success.

The *spirit of helping others* is a key that can open the doors to love,
social connectenesss, and to rewarding customer relationships.

Meditation is a key that can open the doors to the truth of
one's inner nature and to physical calm and mental clarity.

Key Quest

The Inner Journey of the Entrepreneur

Contents

Introduction   7
The Games (Quick Navigation Chart)   14

PART 1: PREPARING FOR YOUR JOURNEY   16

Entrepreneurial Success   16
Key Quest Game Play   17
Six Benefits of Key Quest Game Play   18
Key Quest Game Theory   20
An Inner Practice for your Inner Journey   22
The Spirit of Helping Others   22
Joining an Entrepreneur Community   24

PART 2: THE KEY QUEST SUCCESS MAP   25

Destination Points on the Key Quest Success Map   26
The Five Key Phases of your Success   29
Navigating the Key Quest Success Map   32
⌬ **Game Activity: M-NON (aka Emanon)**   34
The Alternating Principle   35
Accessing Inner Knowledge (Idea Mining)   36
Inner Knowledge Examples from History   36
Inner Reality References   38

PART 3: THE FOUR RINGS OF POSITIVE INFLUENCE 39

Positive Influence   40
The First Ring: Commitment (Enthusiasm)   40
The Second Ring: Compassion (Helping Others)   41
The Third Ring: Confidence (Knowledge)   41
The Fourth Ring: Composure (Integrity)   45

⸻ **Game Activity: PIE Chart**   46

The Diamond Metaphor   47
Staying True   48
PIE Chart Options   50

PART 4: KEYHOLDER MEDITATION FOR ENTREPRENEURS   51

How to Practice Keyholder Meditation for Entrepreneurs   57
The Key Modules   59

⸻ **Game: The Eternal Clock**   107

The 'Set' of 108 Key Questions   108
The Sequential Course/Syllabus Option   108

⸻ **Game: The Year of the Entrepreneur**   109

⸻ **Game: Master Key**   112

The Dice Rolls for *The Eternal Clock* and *Master Key*   113

PART 5: YOUR BRAND VENTURE   125

⸻ **Game: Keys to Adventure**   131

Keys to Adventure Card List   133

PART 6: KEY POINTS ON YOUR JOURNEY   137

⸻ **Game: Time Portal**   140

Timeline Presentations List   142

PART 7: KEY TOPICS   146

Key Topic List   147
Choosing your Topic   151
Finding your Ideas   152
Meditation and Reading   152
New Topics, New Knowledge, Higher Success   154
- **Game: Search for Hidden Treasure (aka Roll & Scroll)**   155

The Dice Rolls for *Search for Hidden Treasure*   156

PART 8: KEY INSIGHTS   192

The Key Insights List   194
- **Game: 21 GEMs**   197

The Key Insights   198

PART 9: KEY QUALITIES   236

The Inner Marathon Milestone Qualities
The Fable of the Inner Marathon   237
An Inner Marathon Bedtime Practice   239
Classification of the 26 Key Qualities   239
- **Game: The Inner Marathon**   240

The Key Qualities   241

PART 10: THE INNER JOURNEY OF THE ENTREPRENEUR   267

The Inner Journey of the Entrepreneur as a Process and as a Game   272
- **Game: The Hero's Journey**   273

The Hero's Journey Card Values   274
- **Game: Key Quotes**   277

An Entrepreneur Wish

*May your happiness grow
and your worries fade,
as you take the things you know
and take the things you've made,
and bring them to the world
to make it a better place.*

*May peace, love, and truth expand,
as you help the world
with your caring brand.*

Dedicated to
my wife and sons

Acknowledgement and Gratitude

*To our compassionate,
purpose-centered entrepreneurs,
and those who support them.*

Introduction

A Blend of Entrepreneurship and Meditation

If you're an entrepreneur who is also interested in the practice of meditation, I have written a book for you, and I also have some very good news for you. The book is ***Key Quest – The Inner Journey of the Entrepreneur***. And the good news is that when you blend the art of entrepreneurship and the practice of meditation in ways that are explained in the book, you access an amazing power that can transport you to a higher reality where your goals are achieved in the easiest and most personally beneficial way possible. How exactly does this happen?

When you blend the many benefits of meditation with the many benefits of being an entrepreneur, the combination opens a powerful door to your inner self, where you can bring your higher inner intelligence and intuition into your decisions and actions. The result is that you make the precise moves that are in your best interest, not only to grow your brand, but also to focus your inner self, and enhance your inner reality. When you exist both within the inner dimension of meditative insight and the outer dimension of your everyday goals, an intriguing effect occurs, intimated in theories of both quantum physics and metaphysics. Essentially, a new multi-dimensional reality is created in which you no longer have to *try* to 'succeed'. Success happens as a natural process emerging from your discovery and following of your personal destiny.

Key Quest is your guide through this reality.

The 10 Parts of the Book

Here are the 10 parts of **Key Quest**, followed by a suggestion on how to travel through its pages:

1. Preparing for your Inner Journey
2. The Key Quest Success Map
3. The Four Rings of Positive Influence
4. Keyholder Meditation for Entrepreneurs
5. Your Brand Venture
6. Key Points on your Journey
7. Key Topics
8. Key Insights
9. Key Qualities
10. The Inner Journey of the Entrepreneur

A Suggestion on how to use Key Quest

The suggestion is to completely read through the first two parts, which will clarify your purpose, vision, and goals, and prepare you to use 'the keys' to 'open the doors' within the book. You can then opt to glance over the rest of the book, intuitively choosing which parts and sections are most important to you at the moment. This will tailor the book specifically to where your motivation to learn will be strongest, and your application to your purpose and brand will be most effective. Of course, you can also read the book in the order it is presented, as I designed it to be an entrepreneurial 'curriculum' following a natural sequence.

You can learn more about my work, along with my free online *Keyholder Meditation Course* on my website, *tonyrubbo.com*.

Now, regarding *this* book, *Key Quest – The Inner Journey of the Entrepreneur,* although I am *teaching* the art of entrepreneurship, I am, and always will be, a *student* of entrepreneurship. It is my background in the field of education and my love for writing that makes it natural for me share my interest in the form of books that teach. So, as for this book, it is intended as a reliable 'curriculum' for those who are opting not to pursue a $20,000 to $40,000 formal college entrepreneurship education. And as for the benefits of *Key Quest*, search *'benefits of meditation', and 'benefits of entrepreneurship'* and blend them to get an idea of the powerful inner door they can open for you.

And regarding the *importance* of entrepreneurship, I think its ultimate value is in the mission that the entrepreneur is advocating through their brand - from the very positive impact they can make in people's lives - all the way to the potential for their brand to save lives. Now as we live and grow, we learn that 'saving a life' can mean many things.

When we see a young person die from a drug overdose, we learn that saving a life could mean relieving someone of a depression that appears to have no solution other than to deaden their experience of life.

When we see someone die of a disease, we might learn that saving a life could mean providing someone with healthier alternatives in their life. Or it could mean supporting a charity that is fighting the disease.

When we see someone die of loneliness, we realize that saving a life can mean being a friend.

When we see someone die from social injustice, we realize that saving a life could mean *advocating* for justice.

I wrote this book for people who look at the world, feel its pain, and want to somehow be a part of lessening the pain. I wrote this book for you - the socially conscious entrepreneur who wants to make a positive change in the world. Now I'd like to share a personal experience that keeps me focused on the feeling of having a mission.

So, my own entrepreneurial journey began with a *service* - helping schools to reach their goals by providing various workshops, programs, and sometimes serving in a school staff function myself. The services I provided to schools turned into books. And so, I then had *products*. And then from the books, I produced other *content* in the form of magazine articles, podcasts, and derivative programs. But of all the services, products, and content I've developed and provided, two memories stand out for me.

The first involves my work in a high school, providing a workshop in which students identified their priorities so they could have clarity on which goals or areas were most important to address. The principal thought it was a very valuable program. She sat in on the workshop and asked me to provide her with the names of students who chose certain topics that might indicate the need for counseling. There was a student who was painfully introverted. In the program, he was able to get in touch with his true feelings and share them with the class. In response, his classmates gave him encouragement and genuine compliments. He was surprised to hear how others truly felt about him. So, within the short period of the workshop, he went from feeling painfully insecure and isolated, to becoming self-confident and popular with his entire class.

> So, sometimes you do good,
> and don't see the actual result.
> It might happen later for the person you helped.
>
> And sometimes you have the good fortune
> of seeing the good result, with the realization that
> it was indeed *you* who made the difference.

There is one more memory that stays with me, and that I'd like to share.

I was providing one of my programs to a youth sports league for young athletes and their families, that involved traits and skills that support an athlete's life and life in general, as well as challenges they might face. The name in this story has been changed for confidentiality.

Kimberly was a high achiever. She was feeling the stress that many young teenagers feel in today's world. But for some reason, Kimberly felt it more deeply. There were so many pressures. People expected a lot from her, and she would never want to disappoint them.

Kimberly's mom had just received a promotion in her career. She was happy that she could be a good female role model for her daughter. She had work stress, but didn't let her daughter see it. Kimberly and her mom participated in my personal-priorities based program.

Kimberly's mom chose a skill-related topic, *'When you manage your time'* as her top priority topic of personal interest. So, she finally shared with her daughter that she was feeling a little pressured by her new assignment.

Kimberly chose a challenge-related topic, *'When you feel like giving up'* as her top choice. When she explained her choice to her mom, Kimberly broke down crying. Her mother was startled and hugged her daughter. Kimberly told her mom how pressured she felt, and that sometimes she saw no way out of her problems.

Her mom just listened, and for the first time, realized that her daughter had been living a life of quiet desperation. She then also began to cry. They talked and talked, and Kimberly shared all the things she had been keeping bottled up for the last year or so. Kimberly and her mom realized how much they still needed each other on that day. Now, Kimberly's mom no longer hides her work-related stressful feelings from her daughter, and Kimberly no longer hides her feelings from her mom. Kimberly and her mom both decided to see a counselor together.

And so, 'saving' a life can mean many things.

I'll share just one more story - of an entrepreneur and her partner whose mission is to provide healthy eating alternatives, especially in the area of sweets. Their sense of mission took on an even greater personal meaning when a customer went out of their way to contact them to share how their health *and their life* changed when they added their nutritious foods to their diet. This is an example of a brand with a clear mission, and of having the good fortune to know the good we are doing by hearing it directly from the people we are helping. **I feel that every purpose-centered and compassionate entrepreneur deserves to have such affirming experiences in their life. This is what I want for *you* ... throughout *your* journey!**

As you are reading this book, you will be reminded that when you keep *your own* sense of mission uppermost in your mind and heart, it transforms your entrepreneurial pursuit into a most personally meaningful inner journey. For as you commit to your purpose and to achieving your goals, you find that you *are* making the world a better place – and realize more and more that the true meaning of life is about values like compassion, kindness, social responsibility, empathy, altruism, and all those qualities that affirm our spirit of helping others.

So, we are entrepreneurs, compassionate and purposeful … and this book is for us. I hope you find that it lives up to all that I want it to be for y<u>ou</u>.

And what I want is for this book to support you in experiencing a sense of physical ease, mental clarity, emotional calm and resiliency, and a deep inner peace as your goals are being set and achieved, as relationships are being developed, and as the entrepreneurial character you are creating and engaging moves through the various settings, scenes, and situations of your life. And so, what I want is for this book to be *extraordinarily* supportive.

And finally, I also want this book to be entertaining!

And regarding the entertainment aspect, the ideas in Key Quest are also presented in entrepreneurial games and game activities. You can use dice, playing cards, a spinning wheel - or an *online* dice, card, or wheel randomizer. Or you can simply self-select your items.

You'll find The Games and Game Activities quick navigation chart on the next two pages.

The Games and Game Activities

Use this chart for quick navigation to a game/activity.

♥ ♠ ♦ ♣	**The Hero's Journey.** The card game of **13 steps on the Inner Journey of the Entrepreneur** correlating to the Hero's Journey mythology and the 13 playing card values. (Part 10)
⊗	**The Inner Marathon.** The self-selection or wheel game of **26 Key Qualities** that support personal development, and doing a monolog or performance. (Part 9)
⚀ ⚁	**The Eternal Clock.** The game of the eternal **12 Key Areas** of Entrepreneurship and answering Key Questions determined by dice rolls. (Part 4)
⊗	**Time Portal.** The self-selection or roulette wheel game of seven **Key Points (timelines) in your Journey,** that involves you giving a presentation on your selection, and giving or receiving a score. (Part 6)
⚀ ⚁ ⚂	**Search for Hidden Treasure (aka Roll & Scroll).** The fast-paced game of internet-searching for Key Points and Ideas on one of the **216 Key Topics** determined by a dice roll of three dice. (Part 7)
🗣	**Key Quotes.** A game activity of giving an **entrepreneurial-themed performance** based on a movie or song quote. (Part 10)

The Games and Game Activities

Use this chart for quick navigation to a game/activity.

	21 GEMs. ("Great Entrepreneurship Means") The self-selection or wheel game involving **21 Key Insights** for your inner journey and success as an entrepreneur. (Part 8)
	Keys to Adventure. The card game with the 52 cards correlating to **52 Key Questions** a venture capitalist might ask. (Part 5)
	PIE Chart. The Positive Influencer Excellence game activity that involves presenting one's brand, product, service, or content and being evaluated on the **Four Rings of Positive Influence**. (Part 3)
	Master Key. A variation on the *Eternal Clock Game* featuring the **12 Key Areas of Entrepreneurship** and answering Key Questions determined by dice rolls. (Part 4)
	M-NON (aka Emanon). The game activity based on the idea mining practice of **Meditation, Notation, Operation, and Notation**, with a business simulation in the operation phase. (Part 2)
	The Year of the Entrepreneur. The game activity that involves notable people, the **12 Key Areas of Entrepreneurship**, and the 12 months of the year. (Part 4)

Part One
Preparing for your Journey

Key Quest is designed to provide a direct path to your success as a compassionate and purpose-centered entrepreneur. Here in Part One, we will prepare for the journey with some travel companion ideas, such as:

- Practical preparation for your entrepreneurial success.
- Key Quest game play and six benefits.
- Adopting an inner practice for your inner journey.
- The value of joining an entrepreneur community.
- The spirit of helping others.

Entrepreneurial Success

- Entrepreneurial success begins with defining **what you are counting** on your journey. (Sales, dollars, customers, readers, listeners, students, subscribers, views, etc.).

- Then locating **where you are currently** in the count.

- And then, **choosing a goal** as a destination. It could be 50 regular clients, 500 monthly paying subscribers, 50,000 customers, 100,000 readers, a million to ten billion views, an initial $100,000 in sales, etc.

Once you have this clarity, it's about applying the key ideas of the book, and engaging in the game activities that support reaching your goal(s). Key Ideas include using the *Key Quest Success Map*, the Inner Practice of *Keyholder Meditation* for your inner journey, along with *Key Traits and Skills, Key Qualities, Key Topics,* and *Key Insights* to assure your entrepreneurial success.

Key Quest Game Play

One of our favorite pastimes is playing games!

We all love to play games of one kind or another, whether it's a video or VR game, a board game, a card game, a dice game. Then there are games shows that involve spinning a wheel, answering questions, etc. And then there is our interest in sports – games that people seem to like watching as much as they like playing!

Some games just bring us pure pleasure. Some are exciting. Some inspire us. And then there are those games that provide us with learning. If you were to research the types of board games alone, you might be surprised at the number and range of topics. It is safe to say that almost every subject, topic, or area of interest has a game of some kind representing it.

Key Quest includes twelve games and game activities supporting the inner journey of the entrepreneur.

See 'The Games – Quick Navigation Chart' following the Introduction for descriptions. And you can search, 'how companies use gamification' to discover how games and game theory are being used in various types of enterprises to support their organizational productivity, training, recruitment, evaluation, etc.

The games involve answering questions, giving performances, and searching for Key Ideas. If you have a repeat roll, spin, or card draw, you can dive deeper and elaborate on your answer, performance, or search.

Six Benefits of Key Quest Game Play

Here are six benefits of using the game formats:

1. A forum for learning, idea-mining, and brain-storming. When you play Key Quest games with partners or with a team, your answers, findings, or performance can support learning, and stimulate a greater range of ideas to support your campaign, purpose, company, brand. Also, consider using a digital assistant to define terms, explain concepts, and for general support.

2. An approach to developing public speaking skills. When you play with someone, your co-player (co-op or cooperative player) serves as your audience, and can share their thoughts on your performance. As you get comfortable with *what* you are communicating, you then develop *how* you are communicating, adding phrasing, inflection, emphasis, intonation, and body language to build your speaking skill.

3. A relationship enhancer. When you play with a friend, relative, or significant other, two things happen. You get to share something that is important to you. And they get to know more about something that is important to you. Sharing of oneself and truly listening or giving one's full attention to another can do wonders for any relationship. And if you are sharing with your significant other about your entrepreneurship and how it may impact your financial status, there is the added motivation that being supportive can also improve your shared situation. Plus, your significant other might have insights of their own regarding ideas or your answers to questions.

4. Game-player enjoyment and benefits. Game-playing releases the body's feel-good chemicals, creating a sense of happiness and well-being. And the idea of turning a real-life entrepreneurial pursuit into a fun casual activity can make the real-life pursuit feel more like fun! With this new positive experience of entrepreneurship comes enhanced creativity and confidence.

5. Game-Playing Magic. We are all familiar with the person at a dice table shaking a pair of dice, blowing on them, and calling out their number as if the energy they put into it will influence the roll. Then there are the people that are cheering. Blowing on dice, calling out the number energetically, people cheering. There is a sense that we can actually influence our fate with the pure power of our desire and intention. So, if you'd like to have this kind of fun, state your purpose intentionally to yourself or out loud before you play. Imagine that you are transferring the energy of your purpose to the dice or wheel, or cards. And play with the feeling that there is a magical quality guiding your play.

6. Game show enjoyment and benefits. Here is a way to turn your game into a game *show*! First you need the contestants. So, two or three people can be the players. Then two or three other people can be the judges who determine who performed or answered their questions best. The judges write their choices. With the multiple judges writing their choices, the players don't know who chose who won and who lost unless they all chose the same winner. And you can even have a host who reads the topics and asks the questions! And of course, you can 'produce' your 'show' on audio or video!

Key Quest Game Theory

Key Quest Game theory offers explanations of how Key Quest games and game activities relate to areas of your life as an entrepreneur. This can help you to determine which area(s) you want to address and focus on their development through game play activity.

Here are the entrepreneurial areas, followed by their Key Quest games and game activities:

Area: Achieving entrepreneurial goals using the practice of meditation as a support.
Game/Activity: M-NON (aka Emanon)

Area: Developing entrepreneurial influence speaking skills.
Game/Activity: PIE Chart

Area: Advancing in the 12 areas of entrepreneurship, including goal-setting, planning, time-management, etc.
Games/Activities: The Eternal Clock, Master Key, The Year of the Entrepreneur

Area: Developing a business/personal plan. Preparing to pitch/present your brand.
Game/Activity: Time Portal

Area: Self-development and entrepreneur-development.
Game/Activity: The Inner Marathon

Areas: Preparing to pitch/present your brand, writing your business plan, developing your brand story talking points.
Game/Activity: Keys to Adventure

Area: Supporting and resolving specific entrepreneurial situations and challenges using the power of affirmation.

Game/Activity: Key Quotes

Area: Researching entrepreneurial topics online and applying them to yourself, your brand, your company.

Game/Activity: Search for Hidden Treasure (aka Roll & Scroll)

Area: Exploring and applying practical as well as inspirational insights supporting your life as an entrepreneur.

Game/Activity: 21 GEMs

Area: Reflecting on your life story as it relates to your entrepreneurial development.

Game/Activity: The Hero's Journey

Also, in this book, supporting the game activities, you will find:

- **The Key Quest Success Map**
  The Key Quest Success Map represents the real-world gameboard of the real-life game of entrepreneurship. So, navigating the Key Quest Success Map naturally connects to all the Key Quest games.

- **Keyholder Meditation for Entrepreneurs**
  Key Meditation for Entrepreneurs is a mantra-based practice on the 12 Key Areas of Entrepreneurship featured in the games: *The Eternal Clock*, *Master Key*, and *The Year of the Entrepreneur*.

An Inner Practice for your Inner Journey

Also, as a reader of this book, you most likely have learned to rely deeply on your intuition to know which decisions are the right ones and that represent your integrity and the true spirit of helping others. To stay in touch with your intuitive or inner nature, you are also most likely interested in the inner practice of Meditation for its many practical applications and nurturing benefits.

By practicing Meditation, you can access your inner self, where you can find or deepen your purpose, access your intuitive nature and your true spirit of helping others. And the reason that you find your spirit of helping others is that the practice of meditation lifts you beyond negative ego needs. And without these ego needs, you are naturally inclined to follow your inner nature to fulfill needs of others – again, to improve their lives, relieve their suffering and pain, etc.

The Spirit of Helping Others

Whether we are just beginning to grow our brand, are further along, or have already achieved extraordinary successes, Key Quest connects us to our spirit of helping others in a way that brings more personal meaning into our activities and accomplishments. For those of us who have achieved all or most of our material goals and are now on a mission of giving back, there is still the idea of *growing* a mission and helping more and more people. And so, Key Quest is also for those of us who are devoting more of our time to charitable work that helps others in personally meaningful ways.

And finally, there are those of us who are blending our purpose with a mission of giving back by making a donation or giving a free product to someone who is in need every time one of our products is purchased.

And so, there is this new, higher kind of entrepreneur that has emerged, and you are one of them. These are entrepreneurs who are striving to make our world a better place by focusing on values like compassion, kindness, inclusivity, social justice, sustainability, wellness, environmental responsibility. When these entrepreneurs are evaluated purely by their rate of progress in a material success perspective, the essential point is missed. And the essential point is that they represent a blend of traditional success *and* social responsibility. As pioneers in a world where traditional material success is still a dominant motivation, their journey may become nontraditional.

Of course, there *will be* those new entrepreneurs who manage their brands very well and excel. Then there will be those who make a living, and those who make a very good living. And then there will be those who sacrifice much to stay the course in their spirit of helping others.

Whatever the rate of progress from very slow to very rapid, these pioneer entrepreneurs represent the hope for humanity's future in the positive values they represent. We can also consider that those who are moving *very* slowly may be spending more time on understanding the human condition, so that when they *do* succeed, it will be of the very highest type of success, positively impacting and advancing the human condition in extraordinarily positive ways.

So, this book is for entrepreneurs who are interested in deepening their commitment to their purpose, their spirit of helping others, and their practice of meditation to access their inner self. This book is for the entrepreneur on an *inner* journey.

Joining an Entrepreneur Community

In the spirit of helping others, you may also be interested in being part of a community of entrepreneurs who share your values of making the world a better place. There are a number of entrepreneurial communities, and you can find one or more that feel right for you. You can also form or join a community that applies ideas from this book, practices Keyholder Meditation, engages in the Key Quest games, etc.

Part Two
Your Key Quest Success Map

The Key Quest Success Map is a tracking platform that features 28 Levels of Success, arranged in 10 stages, and ranging from 1 to 10 billion. Regarding game theory, it represents your real-world entrepreneurial gameboard.

So, the purpose of the Key Quest Success Map is to support your journey from your current level or stage to a significant goal. In the process, you will:

- define what you are counting on your journey (sales, dollars, customers, clients, readers, listeners, subscribers, students, followers, views, etc.).
- locate where you are currently in the count.
- choose an initial or longer-range goal as a destination. It could be 50 regular clients, 500 monthly paying subscribers, 50,000 customers, 100,000 readers, a million to ten billion views, an initial $100,000 in sales.

While you are navigating the levels and stages toward your goal, you can use key ideas from the book, along with ideas that emerge in your meditation. Regarding the Meditation connection, as we know, both practices of Meditation and Entrepreneurship are growing in popularity. With Key Quest, the two practices merge as you advance through levels and stages of outer success while you are deepening your inner meditative lifestyle. And as entrepreneurial ideas emerge through your meditation, they become 'key' ideas when they open the door to each new level of your brand success.

Destination Points on the Key Quest Success Map

Here are examples of goals or destination points on the Key Quest Success Map, presented as levels within stages. So, begin by defining *what you are counting.* This relates to who you are as an entrepreneur, or as someone who practices and applies entrepreneurial skills. For example, if you are a product creator or distributor, the number might be customers or sales. If you are a content creator, the number might be views. If you are an actor, athlete, performer, celebrity, etc., the number might be your fan base. If you are an author, columnist, or writer in any capacity, your number might be readers or circulation. If you operate a non-profit, the number might be patrons. And the list goes on, regarding 'types' of entrepreneurs.

Stage 1: (Levels 1 through 4)

Level #	Level Achievement
1	1 - 10
2	10 - 25
3	25 - 50
4	50 - 100

Stage 2: Levels 5 through 7

Level #	Level Achievement
5	100 - 250
6	250 - 500
7	500 - 1,000

Stage 3: Levels 8 through 10

Level #	Level Achievement
8	1,000 - 2,500
9	2,500 - 5,000
10	5,000 - 10,000

Stage 4: Levels 11 through 13

Level #	Level Achievement
11	10,000 - 25,000
12	25,000 - 50,000
13	50,000 - 100,000

Stage 5: Levels 14 through 17

Level #	Level Achievement
14	100,000 - 250,000
15	250,000 - 500,000
16	500,000 - 1 million

Imagine Level 16 and its total of 1 million. Now think about Level 1, and its total of ten. The value of using the Key Quest Success Map is that it lays out a seamless sequence through all quantities, and it keeps us inspired, motivated, in the moment, and grounded in our intention of helping others. With this in mind, take a moment to define *where you are currently in your count,* and *a short, medium, or long-range goal (destination point).*

Stage 6: Levels 17 through 19

Level #	Level Achievement
17	1 million - 2.5 million
18	2.5 million - 5 million
19	5 million - 10 million

Stage 7: Levels 20 through 22

Level #	Level Achievement
20	10 million - 25 million
21	25 million - 50 million
22	50 million - 100 million

Stage 8: Levels 23 through 25

Level #	Level Achievement
23	100 million - 250 million
24	250 million - 500 million
25	500 million - 1 billion

Stage 9: Levels 26 through 28

Level #	Level Achievement
26	1 billion - 2.5 billion
27	2.5 billion - 5 billion
28	5 billion - 10 billion

The Five Key Phases of your Success

Besides knowing the specific stages and levels of our journey, it can be helpful to know general phases. So, here are five key phases of success.

Prelaunch: If your product, service, content, etc. has not yet been made available for purchase or use, you are in the Prelaunch phase. While in prelaunch, you can choose a stage and/or level as an initial destination and use its number to provide inspiration, ideas, insights, and direction regarding what you are doing to prepare. In this way, you can test ideas against the realities that will be emerging on the way to your goals. When your product, service, or content achieves the quality that fully supports your destination, you are ready to launch. So, the prelaunch stage is essentially about adjustment, refinement, possibly testing the market with interviews, surveys, etc. and going as deep as possible and feasible to understand your quest from launch to your destination. You might define elements within your prelaunch, such as product creation, production, distribution channels, marketing campaigns, order fulfillment, etc.

You might also want to project your thinking into further future stages and levels to understand what they will involve and how they transition. In the process, you may be surprised at how much is actually involved in your quest. When you finally do launch, then what you have discovered or developed in the prelaunch stage will be laid out ahead of you as goals. And all the gems of wisdom that you have uncovered will be used when challenges arise that require innovative ideas and solutions.

So, settle in and realize that your relentless mental activity in the prelaunch stage will eventually give way to a sense of organization and structure once you launch. It's been said that the entrepreneur works 80 hours a week so they don't have to work 40. And that's why the journey of the entrepreneur is a hero's quest. The hero lives, sleeps, and breathes their purpose - their desire to bring something genuinely good to the world. Welcome to your Key Quest.

Launch: Once you have prepared in the Prelaunch phase, you are ready for the Launch phase, which includes:

- Offering your product, service, or content for sale. Monitoring the results. Adjusting based on the results.
- Developing and strengthening in the areas of entrepreneurship, such as goal-setting, planning, organization, time-management, skill-development, problem-solving, communication, and leadership.
- Growing in the spirit of helping others, and developing the ability to positively influence people.

Growth: Then the Growth phase, which includes:

- Engaging in a practice such as meditation for ideas on how to advance your mission and purpose, besides accruing the physical, mental, and other benefits.
- Proving the concept and growing the brand.
- Deepening the spirit of helping others by seeing how what you are providing is actually helping others.
- Forming mutually rewarding relationships to support the purpose, brand, and spirit of helping others.
- Clarifying the customer journey for smooth operation so that scaling will be a seamless transition.

Expansion: On to the Expansion phase, which includes:

- Increasing sales with less addition of resources than in the growth phase.
- Having identified a clear substantial market, developing ideas on how to reach that market and take the product, service, or content to the masses.
- Identifying and unlocking new markets and reaching new audiences.
- The realization that having a good system in place is extremely important when it comes to managing the activities and challenges of expansion.
- Engaging in the inner practice of meditation to reflect on what's working and what's not, and to discover insights in the meditative state that reveal strategies on how to achieve more with less effort.

Maturity: And finally, the Maturity phase, which includes:

- Your brand, product, service, and/or content becoming part of the culture and helping people in all the ways that it is intended to do so.
- Developing a self-image of being a helper and a positive force for humanity.
- Experiencing both the outer maturity of the brand success and the inner maturity of inner practice mastery.
- Your inner journey continuing with the pursuit of accessing and experiencing your innermost nature, and bringing the insights and benefits of your inner experience into the course of everyday life.

In each phase, the entrepreneur on an inner journey will find benefits in being part of an entrepreneur community. For example: entrepreneurs who are in the same phase support each other by comparing their notes; where entrepreneurs who are in a more advanced phase support those who are in an earlier phase, and members who are in an earlier phase are supported by those in a later, more advanced phase.

Navigating the Key Quest Success Map

Since this is an *inner* journey, moving from one point to another on the map involves the inner practice of meditation and the application of ideas that emerge from your practice. This process involves: 1) Mining for ideas, 2) Making notes, 3) Taking action, and 4) Assessing results. And here is the breakdown:

Mining for ideas (Meditate)
Going into a meditative state (meditation, contemplation, reflection, taking quiet time) with the intention of idea mining for your purpose and goal. With your purpose-based goal as a mantra, wait for ideas to emerge. The skill here is to let unrelated thoughts come and go, and settle in on thoughts related to your purpose and goal. And the quality that makes it happen in your idea mining is your meditative receptivity.

Making notes (Notate)
Using a notebook, journal, document, etc. for notes on your Key Quest (your Keynotes), make an entry that captures the key point(s) of your idea(s).

Taking action (Operate)
Implement your idea(s), or imagine implementation.

Assessing results (Notate)
Evaluate how your ideas translated into action and results. Notate your results in your Keynotes.

If you *imagined* implementation, evaluate how your ideas translated into action and results in your simulation.

Use your Keynotes as supportive content when you go back to your meditation. Continue the process.

Make the *Meditation-Notation-Operation-Notation* process (M-NON) a habit, and watch your performance improve and the number of people you are helping increase.

Consider that your Keynotes file or notebook is your own personal success book, based on *your* intuitive thoughts, actions, assessments, and values.

Acknowledge and recognize how valuable your Keynotes are to your success.

M-NON (aka Emanon)

NAME

M-NON (aka Emanon) is a Key Quest game activity, with M-NON referring to the Meditation-Notation-Operation-Notation process. And *Emanon* derives from the idea that when we go deep into meditation, we reach a free, clear state from which intuitive ideas can emerge – a state that has no name. *Emanon* is 'no name' spelled backwards.

(And here's an interesting synchronicity that someone discovered. Check out the name of Greek hero, Agamemnon, and break it down: A game mnon.)

FRAME

The frame of the M-NON Game Activity is that of an idea mining or brainstorming session. The play involves team or group members meditating on a goal and waiting for intuitive ideas to emerge from the meditative state. Ideas are recorded and shared. Members come up with simulations of implementing the ideas, and potential outcomes in the operation of your brand. Insights and their value to your brand are noted and discussed.

AIM

The aim of *the M-NON Game Activity* is to support your brand or company in realizing its goals. As we advance in this activity skill, we discover the Alternating Principle: which states that the more <u>in</u>ward we go, the more positive <u>out</u>comes we can experience. Then, the more positive <u>out</u>comes we experience, the further <u>in</u>ward we can go. And so, a cycle begins, and we advance our purpose by blending our inner-development and our helping others. On the next page, we will look at four examples of the Alternating Principle in practice.

The Alternating Principle

The more <u>in</u>ward we go, the more positive <u>out</u>comes we can experience. Then, the more positive <u>out</u>comes we experience, the further <u>in</u>ward we can go. Here are four examples of the alternating principle in practice.

M-NON to achieve 10 (10 thousand, 10 million, etc.)
Meditate on past learning, any results you've achieved, and practice your meditative receptivity. Note ideas, insights and strategies in your Keynotes and bring them into your operations to achieve ten. Note your activities and outcomes. Continue the process.

M-NON: From 10 to 25 (25 thousand, 25 million, etc.)
Meditate on past learning, any results you've achieved, and practice your meditative receptivity. Note ideas, insights and strategies in your Keynotes and bring them into your operations to achieve another 15, bringing total to 25. Note activities and outcomes. Continue the process.

M-NON: From 25 to 50 (50 thousand, 50 million, etc.)
Meditate on past learning, any results you've achieved, and practice your meditative receptivity. Note ideas, insights and strategies in your Keynotes and bring them into your operations to achieve another 25, bringing your total to 50. Note activities and outcomes. Continue.

M-NON: From 50 to 100 (100 thousand, 100 million, etc.)
Meditate on past learning, any results you've achieved, and practice your meditative receptivity. Note ideas, insights and strategies in your Keynotes and bring them into your operations to achieve another 50, bringing your total to 100. Note activities and outcomes. Continue.

Accessing Inner Knowledge
(to support Idea Mining)

Being an entrepreneur on an inner journey, you may have already intuitively sensed something about the nature of success. And that is that your success as an entrepreneur already exists within you, or is somehow connected to you. It is not something you need to initially invent, but rather something for you to first discover and access. Here we will refer to that *something* as existing in your Higher or Inner Reality, with its definition being *a store of inner knowledge about your life as it relates to your entrepreneurial journey*. Of course, accessing such inner knowledge would be an extraordinary support to the process of idea mining.

And the practice that is perhaps the most direct method to access your higher or inner reality is the inner practice of Meditation.

Inner Knowledge Examples from History

Accessing our **inner knowledge** is a process similar to the meditative or dreamlike process that Albert Einstein used to discover his theories and sublime knowledge, as well as the process of Nikola Tesla and other examples of people we refer to as geniuses. (*Consider that a genius is someone who can think at a higher or deeper level, and that this level of thought can be accessed with meditation, focused daydreaming, nocturnal dreaming, and such sublime states of mind.*) Other examples include the discovery of the periodic table by Dmitri Mendeleev, and the scientific method by René Descartes.

And one of the most compelling accounts of accessing information through a sublime mind state is that of Srinivasa Ramanujan, who had very little formal training in mathematics, but produced almost 4,000 proofs, conjectures and equations in pure mathematics. He shares an experience in which a red screen appeared. He says, *"I was observing it. Suddenly a hand began to write on the screen. I became all attention. That hand wrote a number of elliptic integrals. They stuck to my mind."* After his experience, he recorded them.

So, we know with certainty that there is information and knowledge that can be accessed from higher or inner regions of our reality by people ranging from those like Einstein who possessed an impressive intelligence and degree of knowledge - to those like Ramanujan who possessed very little knowledge on his topic.

Let's consider that Einstein valued science and wanted to understand the truth of how the universe operated, and how to fit it into the structure of the rational scientific mind. A*ffirming* this higher value, he then *accessed* the higher or inner reality related to this value. In other words, he brought himself into attunement with the higher or inner reality by taking purposeful action that resonated with it. And then a new truth of the universe was revealed to him.

The *true* value of *the entrepreneur* is that people are being *truly* helped with their product, service or content. So, *your* inner reality represents the world of your product, service, or content in its ideal state; so your journey would involve opening an inner door to access it.

Inner Reality References

Regarding the higher or inner reality that you access in your meditative or contemplative state, you can choose one of two references. The first is that this higher or inner reality is a place where intuitive thoughts emerge from our own personal deeper or higher intelligence. It can be thought of as bridging the gap between our conscious and nonconscious minds, between instinct and rational thought. We can call this the humanist approach.

The other is that the meditative state is a bridge or door to another dimension of reality. References include the Zero Point Field from quantum physicist, Albert Einstein, or the collective unconscious (which is also known as the 'objective psyche') from psychologist, Carl Jung, etc. Contrasted with the humanist approach, we can refer to this as a universal approach.

Whether humanist or universal, physical or psychological, we know that we can discover ideas, insights, direction, guidance from a place beyond our logical thinking minds. Let's revisit Einstein for some of his quotes:

- "The intellect has little to do on the road to discovery. There comes a leap in consciousness, call it Intuition or what you will, the solution comes to you and you don't know how or why."
- "Logic will get you from A to B. Imagination will take you EVERYWHERE."
- "I think 99 times and find nothing. I stop thinking, swim in silence, and the truth comes to me."

Part Three
The Four Rings of Positive Influence
(The Four C's)

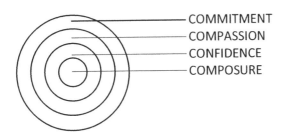

As you are navigating your Key Quest Success Map and transforming your ideas into reality, you will be communicating your values, your brand, your company and your purpose to people – customers, associates, patrons, etc. When you engage the Four Rings of Positive Influence, these people will sense your qualities of:

- Commitment, as you communicate with enthusiasm.
- Compassion, as you communicate in the pure spirit of helping others.
- Confidence, as you share your knowledge of how your product, service, content, or brand helps others.
- Composure, as you communicate from a place of integrity.

When these four qualities are sensed together, the person's entire being is engaged. The energy of enthusiasm is sensed physically. Compassion is sensed emotionally. Confidence and the testimonials appeal to the intellect and are sensed mentally. And the aura of inner calm composure and integrity are sensed intuitively.

Positive Influence

Developing Positive Influence begins with:

1) knowing your product and being totally passionate about its ability to help others, make the world a better place, and provide a desired experience or solution.

2) knowing as much as possible about exactly who your customers are - their interests, their activities, their life. The ultimate situation is when you also use the product yourself and receive the experience and the solution that it provides, since you then are also a customer, and can relate fully to your customers.

The First Ring: Commitment
Communicating with Enthusiasm

The First Ring of Positive Influence involves projecting and transferring your commitment and enthusiasm to another person. This begins with the genuine desire to understand a person's situation and problems, then sharing your commitment to your product, and helping them with your product. Your commitment and enthusiasm are so authentic and energized that it is contagious. So, the customer is not only having their problem solved, they are also having a very empowering and enjoyable experience, which adds to their experience of the product when they bring it into their lives. And of course, if you are a customer of the product yourself, there is the feeling that you are sharing *your own* positive experience and feelings in owning and using the product.

The Second Ring: Compassion
Communicating with the Spirit of Helping Others

In the Second Ring of Positive Influence, you build upon your commitment and enthusiasm with your compassion and pure spirit of helping others. To grasp this idea, we might draw inspiration from the health care professional giving advice to help a patient. There is no sense of selling, there is just the caring for the patient. This is an example of the true spirit of helping others. When you bring this kind of compassion into your purpose, your commitment and enthusiasm are still there, and now your next deeper inner quality is your true spirit of helping your customer.

The Third Ring: Confidence
Communicating with the Knowledge of your Product's Benefits

In the Third Ring of Positive Influence, we experience the confidence that comes from the *knowledge* that our product helps people, and we do this by realizing how our product increases 'positivity' for our customer either directly, or by reducing or removing negativity.

Perhaps, the simplest example of positivity is that *health and wellness* are positive, and *sickness and disease* are negative. And so, if a product, service, content, or brand supports wellness, it is both increasing the positive (wellness), and decreasing the negative (disease). Of course, a product might lean more toward one than the other. For example, a mission might involve helping someone who has been diagnosed with a disease, which would lean toward reducing or removing the negative.

Or it might be representing a nutritional product or exercise program for people in general, not only people diagnosed with disease, which would be more directly focused on the positive.

One perspective on this is that life inherently has pain and suffering, and if we can bring anything positive into a person's life, it is an act of compassion to alleviate this inherent human condition. And this equates to qualities like authentic kindness, genuine friendship, and sincerely caring for the wellbeing of another.

So, we are in the mission of helping 'a friend' in need, and in doing so, being a friend indeed.

Now please take a moment to think about your mission, and your product, service, content, or brand; and consider which of these wants and needs it satisfies:

1. I want to feel safe, secure, protected.
2. I want excitement, adventure.
3. I want approval, recognition, status, a positive image, respect.
4. I want a feeling of social connection, community, friendship.
5. I want health, wellness, a sense of well-being, fitness.
6. I want success, achievement, a sense of purpose.
7. I want to experience victory, triumph, winning.
8. I want growth, development, advancement, education.
9. I want to be financially secure, wealthy, prosperous.
10. I want comfort, ease, peace-of-mind.

11. I want relief from pain, suffering, stress, discomfort.
12. I would like to be admired, well-regarded.
13. I want to have more enjoyment or pleasure in my life.
14. I want to experience luxury, prestige, grandeur, bliss.
15. I want to avoid disapproval, humiliation, shame.
16. I want my life to feel easier.
17. I want feel more efficient and competent in my work.
18. I want to own things that please my senses.
19. I want to own things that please my intellect.
20. I want to own/do things that my friends own/do.

When I buy something, I want to be able to say:

1. I like that it solves my problem.
2. I like its style, its features.
3. I like how it can help me reach my goal.
4. I like that it works reliably.
5. I like how it makes me feel.
6. I like how it makes me look, appear, seem.
7. I like how it makes a function or activity easier.
8. I like how it makes me feel connected to my group.
9. I like it because my valued friends like it.
10. I like what it represents, how it helps the world.

These wants and needs represent positive thoughts, feelings, states, aspirations – either *directly* positive or in how they represent the reduction or removal of negativity. As positivity represents a universal human truth, when your product satisfies such wants and needs, you are aligned to absolute ideals of human nature. There is no doubt; there is only the absolute certainty that your product will bring your customer to (or toward) a quality, state, or experience considered to be beneficial.

So, dive into your products, their features and benefits, and identify what is positive about them, the positive benefits they provide - how they make your customer's life more positive.

This is both *your* truth and a *universal human* truth ... so, this truth prepares you to *communicate* from that place of inner calm composure born of truth and certainty.

When you simply communicate from your truth and your absolute certainty that produces that state of confidence, the sale is still the total focus, but you no longer *worry* about *making* the sale. Your success or achievement is in *your offering* of your product, service, content, or brand. In other words, your confidence comes from the actual knowledge, truth and certainty that you are doing the exact right thing in offering of your product. So, you find yourself communicating and interacting with your customers without ego. You simply share how what you are offering *will* help them.

In this way, you let the responsibility *belong to your prospective customer*s in their doing the right thing for themselves. You don't judge their decision. If they decide on your product, you remain stoic and confident. If they don't decide on your product, you remain stoic and confident, and simply continue on your purpose.

You can deepen your confidence even further by learning directly from customers how they benefited from your product. You can do this by finding customer success stories; checking online reviews and recommendations. And/or you can just ask your own customers directly.

With your knowledge of your customers' testimonials, along with your commitment, your enthusiasm, and your genuine spirit of helping, you now go deeper within yourself to experience confidence in your product ... and yourself. So, you communicate with the absolute knowledge that your product delivers the benefits you are promising. Then your new prospective customers don't see you just as a salesperson, but rather as someone they can genuinely trust. And the testimonials assure even the most skeptical prospective customers that your product can help them in the same way that it has actually helped others, especially if customers providing the testimonials share their names and/or any other personal information.

The Fourth Ring: Composure
Communicating with Integrity

Finally, with the Fourth Ring of Positive Influence, we move toward our innermost source, as we integrate our commitment, compassion, and confidence with our inner nature. With this personal integration, we naturally find our integrity. And with our integrity, comes a sense of composure that is felt intuitively by our customers.

With this integrity that comes the blend of your sense of commitment, your spirit of helping others, and your stoic feeling of confidence, you will naturally grow through stages and levels of success, and your success will come to you commensurate with your inner dedication and spirit. There is no concern. There is no worry. You are simply communicating confidently from truth, and *staying true.*

PIE CHART

NAME

The name, PIE Chart refers to the idea of achieving or aspiring to excellence as a positive influencer, and is based on the Four Rings of Positive Influence. And so, the name PIE is an acronym for Positive Influencer Excellence. And 'Chart' refers to the scoring format.

FRAME

The frame of the PIE Chart game activity is presenting your product, service, content, or brand in either a personal or social setting. The play involves experiencing a blend of enthusiasm based on your commitment to your purpose, a helping spirit based on your compassion, confidence based on your knowledge, and a sense of inner calm composure that comes from your personal integrity.

You evaluate your own performance, or you present in front of others, who evaluate it. Scoring is 1-30 for Commitment, Compassion, and Confidence, and 1-10 for the more sublime quality of Composure, making 100 a perfect score. The following chart represents two players.

Quality/Player	1	2	1 and 2 (Decimal Option)	
Commitment	28	26	2.8	2.6
Compassion	30	29	3.0	2.9
Confidence	26	24	2.6	2.4
Composure	8	7	8.0	7.0
Total	92	86	9.2	8.6

AIM

The aim is for you to further deepen your commitment to your purpose, and increase your positive influence.

The Diamond Metaphor

Now let's look at a metaphor for the Four Rings that might bring a shine to your smile and a sparkle to your eye. And that is because the idea of Four C's is also found in the study of diamonds. The Four C's of a diamond are: Carat weight, Color, Clarity, and Cut. Here are the correlations:

Carat weight correlates to the physicalness of the diamond, and therefore connects to the physical energy found in the first ring of positive influence where enthusiasm is communicated and transferred directly to the customer – The Ring of Commitment.

Color refers to the beauty of the diamond, correlating to the emotions and connecting to the emotional quality of the second ring – The Ring of Compassion.

Clarity refers to the degree of absence of imperfections in the diamond. Surface imperfections are referred to as blemishes, and internal imperfections are inclusions. Mentally, these can refer to distractions, either from the outside or inside. A customer has more clarity and is less distracted when they are assured of the product with testimonials. And so, Clarity connects to the mental clarity found in the third ring – The Ring of Confidence.

Cut refers to the way the diamond's shape has been refined through the cutting of the stone. Cut has the greatest influence on the diamond's shine and sparkle. And the connection is that when we refine ourselves to communicate with full integrity, it has the greatest influence on our state of inner calm, with the fourth and innermost ring being The Ring of Composure.

So, the message is to find your shine. Find your sparkle. Aspire to be a flawless diamond as you refine your traits and skills on your inner journey as a compassionate and purpose-centered entrepreneur.

Staying True

When we have travelled through all four rings of positive influence and are operating from the innermost ring of composure, we can refer to it as *staying true*. It is here that we shine. It is here that we sparkle. To stay true in our purpose of helping others, we focus on just that – the people we are helping with our product/service/content. And this leads us to the Key Quest definition of a sale, which is:

A sale is any time a person
is helped with our product/service/content -
and our purpose of helping others
is further supported by the purchase.

And so, the entrepreneur travels their inner journey focused on one thing – the sale (or related item). Everything else is seen and experienced as it relates to supporting the sale. And a question we might consider every morning for the day ahead is:

How does every person I see or meet, every place I go, everything I utilize, every activity I perform support me in helping others – support the sale?

With this single-pointed mindset, we are bringing the focus we develop in meditation into our purpose. And the result is that we become more focused, more efficient, less distracted – more stoic.

Anything that might have previously captured our attention, created a detour in our journey, distracted us from our purpose in any way is now handled in an entirely *new* way. It is handled in the same way that we handle distractions in our inner practice. And that is that we note the distraction and return our focus – in this case, to the sale and the way what we are doing supports the sale.

Since the sale is a social interaction, distractions are often socially-based. So, as we remain stoic and stay true, we find an empowering process beginning in which our social personality refines itself. Negative traits and feelings are processed in a way that produces self-awareness and self-refinement. Such negative traits and feelings can include: regret, resentment, inadequacy, selfishness, superiority, arrogance, loneliness, inferiority, jealousy, conceit, vanity, narcissism, anger, sadness, fear, and so on. These feelings may be general and vague, or they may have specific memories or worries attached to them.

And besides the emotional distractions, there may be the mental distractions of random thoughts, physical distractions of stress or feeling unhealthy, or existential distractions regarding the meaning of our life, etc.

Through all of it, the entrepreneur on the inner journey remains calm and stoic, stays true, always returning focus to the sale and activities that support the sale. In this way, the entrepreneur's compassionate and purposeful action becomes a meditation practice in itself – a self-refining process - an inner practice. And then, the journey is truly an inner journey based on the spirit of helping others.

PIE CHART Options

The Mission Option: In the Mission Option, you advocate for a social cause with the goal being for the viewer or audience member to be inspired by your commitment, compassion, confidence, and composure to become more aware or to get involved in some way. Presentations can be about a story, an insight, a personal experience, a statistic, etc. regarding the people or challenge related to the mission. Besides *performing*, this option can include *creating* an imaginative video using voiceover, visual elements, music, etc. Rather than score the four qualities, you can opt to simply evaluate the overall impact, using a 1.0 to 10.0 scoring system. The Mission Option can also connect your mission with your brand, if a benefit of your product, service, or content relates to the mission.

The Topic Option: Here the entrepreneur addresses any topic they feel is worth exploring through an inspiring performance or creative video. Examples are social media, cryptocurrency, veganism, love, technology, financial wellness, the blend of entrepreneurship and meditation - essentially any topic that the presenter feels has value.

With our Key Quest Success Map in place,
Key Points defined, Key Ideas in development,
and an understanding of how to access inner knowledge
and develop our positive influence,
we are prepared for a deep dive into
12 Key Areas that support your inner journey
as an *entrepren*eur ... with the practice *of
Keyholder Meditation for Entrepreneurs.*

Part Four
Keyholder Meditation for Entrepreneurs

Keyholder Meditation is a results-oriented practice, suggested by the 'key' idea of using a key to open a door or unlock potential. I've brought Keyholder Meditation to the fields of education, business, and sports with very positive practical results. So, when applied to the field of Entrepreneurship, this inner practice can produce very focused and impressive results in your outer everyday world. On that practical note, here are the 12 Key Areas featured in Keyholder Meditation for Entrepreneurs:

1. The Spirit of Helping Others
2. Goal-Setting
3. Planning
4. Organization
5. Time-Management
6. Skill-Development
7. Problem-Solving
8. Communication
9. Self-Presentation
10. Synergy
11. Leadership
12. Positivity

The practice involves a mantra and content supporting the mantra. The idea is to say the mantra, read the content, and then repeat the mantra as a meditation.

This satisfies both your intellectual and intuitive nature, as the content explains the concept, and the mantra brings its essence into the depths of your innermost nature.

As the trait or skill becomes a natural part of you, you see positive outcomes, which in turn, inspires you to continue cultivating them. This ongoing process of honing and refining brings mastery in the key areas and excellence as a compassionate and purpose-centered entrepreneur.

The following is an example of how the 12 Key Areas flow. As you read it, think of how it applies to your own brand venture. Naturally, you can change the types of people (customers, followers, readers, students, etc.), numbers (sales, dollars, views, etc.), and other details as needed.

1. The Spirit of Helping Others

You begin in the pure spirit of helping others. So, when you make a sale, instead of thinking, "I made a sale", you think, "I've helped someone."

2. Goal-Setting

With your spirit of helping others, you consider how many people you want to help initially, let's say 10,000 people. And your item sells for $20.

3. Planning

With the U.S. representing your initial market population, you consider that if you helped 10,000 people with your product, you would be helping approximately one out of every 33,000 people in the U.S. You consider the goal very possible to accomplish if you can identify and approach those populations within the country who would be most interested and best helped. So, you make your plans.

4. Organization

You begin to organize data regarding the locations of people who would want your product and realize how much simpler the project is since we now have virtual locations that are easily identified and accessed. So, you search online and collect that data. And then you organize yourself, your files, your workspace, and your entire brand to best support your campaign.

5. Time-Management

Next you organize your weeks, your days, and your hours. In other words, you practice time-management and manage your time to support your campaign. You discover new habits to make the best of your time and reduce or remove habits that are not useful or productive.

6. Skill-Development

You realize the skills that you are developing in your goal-setting, planning, and time-management, and consider other skills you will need. There may be skills related to web design, inventory, marketing, order fulfillment, etc.

7. Problem-Solving

So, you begin developing the skills. You learn how to inventory your product and market it, and how to fulfill orders and manage the numbers. You realize that some areas present certain challenges – certain problems.
You see them as indicating your need for new skills. For example, you'll need to learn how to set up your website to offer your product, how to create an online store, how to sell your product through other online platforms, and how to connect to your population through social media.

So, people then purchase your product and share why they like your product, which builds your confidence, while your practice of meditation and your total belief in your product support a very effective state of inner calm.

8. Communication

With a good foundation of knowledge and skills and some initial results, you realize that it's now all about your ability to communicate and to influence people in a positive way and in the spirit of helping others. So, with your commitment, your compassion, your confidence, and your sense of inner calm, you expand your spoken and written communication-skills, including in-person, phone, videoconferencing, email, social-media; and you stay current with any new emerging communication technologies.

9. Self-Presentation

As you continue to practice and improve your spoken and written communication skills, you realize that there is another aspect to communicating that can further expand your influence, your likeability, and the acceptance and trust that people have in what you are saying. In other words, the way that you present yourself. So, you look objectively at yourself and you change this, adjust that, fine-tune your social image, and become adept at the fine art of self-presentation.

10. Synergy

Up to this point, it has mainly been about you. As you are getting to know yourself better, you reach a new point where you are ready to know others in a new way.

You are ready to experience the full power of synergy and the art of creative cooperation. You look at populations, your customers, your potential customers, your suppliers, people who support operations, production, marketing, sales, accounting, and finance, etc. You see how they all support the success of your mission, and how when their efforts are aligned and coordinated, the overall productivity increases.

You begin to develop new relationships with influencers and marketing affiliates who earn income by referring people to your brand and product. You form a synergistic team designed so that when one succeeds, the entire team succeeds. You learn the amazing power of synergy and dedicate yourself to bringing as much synergy into your brand operations as possible.

11. Leadership

With your understanding of your role and the roles of others, you begin developing or strengthening your leadership skills. You learn to develop a comprehensive vision for your brand and strategic planning to support it. And so, your team grows, your sales grow, the number of people you are helping grows. You become more and more authentic until you are communicating with complete transparency, securing your status as a leader in your field. You learn to recognize those whom you want to be part of your team, and which tasks to delegate to whom. You become a role model of your brand and your brand values. You learn how to find answers and advice to support ongoing growth. Finally, you support your team members to become leaders themselves.

12. Positivity

With your foundation of entrepreneurial leadership, you move from thinking about your product and about your product's personality to thinking about your system. With systems thinking, you see how all the parts of your brand and company connect and affect one other. You realize that when you bring positivity to the separate parts, together they bring positive movement to the whole.

With this overall system positivity, your brand and company now have a foundation that will support growth, expansion, scaling. And with this foundation of positivity, you instinctively recognize driving (positive) forces that support your brand and restraining (negative) forces that can hinder your brand. You become more proactive (positive) in your decision-making, and less reactive (negative), not reacting to challenges by making impulsive choices that don't consider the big picture.

You realize that there is a duality, and a binary decision to be made at every point in the inner journey of the entrepreneur. And that is whether the decision or action will result in positive movement or negative movement. As a compassionate, purpose-centered entrepreneur who practices meditation, and has a mission to help others and make the world a better place, you intuitively know what makes a decision truly positive. This is your advantage. This is your gift.

How to Practice
Keyholder Meditation for Entrepreneurs

1. Read the mantra statement at the top of each page for awareness and understanding.

2. Read the page. Choose one or more of the following:
   - Let key ideas enter a deeper part of you.
   - Highlight or underline keywords and phrases.
   - Record your thoughts in your Keynotes.

3. Then go back to the mantra statement and meditate on it aloud, in a whisper, or silently. As you repeat it, you will naturally move from understanding, to appreciation, to acceptance, and finally to preparing to adopt it for use on your entrepreneurial journey.

When you do bring it into the journey of your everyday entrepreneurial activities, you will be developing the quality or skill in a practical sense. And then you will naturally grow the quality or skill as you alternate between your mantra meditation and your entrepreneurial application.

To use *Keyholder Meditation for Entrepreneurs* as a sequential course or syllabus, you can go through the 48 Key Modules in the order they are presented, as they are arranged to follow a natural developmental progression.

Or you can tailor the course to your needs with the following approach:

1. Look over the 12 Key Areas

> 1. The Spirit of Helping Others
> 2. Goal-Setting
> 3. Planning
> 4. Organization
> 5. Time-Management
> 6. Skill-Development
> 7. Problem-Solving
> 8. Communication
> 9. Self-Presentation
> 10. Synergy
> 11. Leadership
> 12. Positivity

2. Choose the area that feels most important to you at the moment.

3. Look over that area's mantras.

4. Intuitively choose one.

5. Meditate on the mantra and module.

6. Read the next intuitively chosen mantra from that area, or choose the next most important area, and continue the process.

Following the 48 Key Modules are three games based on Keyholder Meditation for Entrepreneurs: *The Eternal Clock, The Year of the Entrepreneur,* and *Master Key.*

The Spirit of Helping Others
- Key Module 1 -

*My customers and I are similar
since we share the same values
of my product (service, content).
So, being of help to them feels natural and right.*

Think about the fact that you are an individual in a society of other individuals. You are both singular and collective, a unique person, and a member of a community. You are different than others and you are similar to others. In this meditation module, we will consider that the spirit of helping others deepens by identifying certain similarities. These are similarities inherent in your purpose, vision, goals, and your feelings about your purpose. When you are in the company of people who want those things that represent what you have to offer - people who share your deepest feelings about its value in one's life, the spirit of helping others feels natural and right.

When we think of a brand or a company, we might not automatically think of the people that are being helped by its product, service, content, etc., but they are what essentially defines the brand or company. So, the essential role of our brand or company is to serve other people – customers, clients, patrons, readers, students, listeners, viewers, etc. In other words, consumers of the products, services, or content that we provide. As we value what we offer, so do they. And so, we are kindred spirits, and our brand brings us together.

The Spirit of Helping Others
- Key Module 2 -

***As an entrepreneur,
I am in the pure spirit of helping others
with my product/service/content.***

The Spirit of Helping Others begins with going from self-consciousness to other-consciousness. And this involves dropping the concerns of the conditioned human self, for the awareness, understanding and appreciation of the concerns and needs of others. Your body then becomes an instrument of service, and you use it to support the person (or people) you are serving. Your mind (in its ability to think, plan, make decisions, etc.) also becomes such an instrument for helping others.

This doesn't suggest that you are doing something for others because you think you're a good person, since this would indicate ego attachment and produce more ego material to be resolved. On the inner path, the spirit of helping others means doing something in the service of others without a clinging need for acknowledgement or ego gratification. When you let go of your conditioned identity and its ego concerns and give yourself to fully supporting and fulfilling the needs of another, it is simply a sign that you are transcending your ego, and your true higher nature is being accessed. When this giving spirit is fulfilled, you naturally receive (payment). However, it is a higher kind of receiving, without a grasping sense to it, since you are so centered in the stoic helping spirit.

The Spirit of Helping Others
- Key Module 3 -

**I am replacing any self-serving,
fear-based, weaker perspectives
with the compassion-based,
stronger perspective of helping others.**

Consider that customers, clients, consumers of your products, services, content, or brand are people who need something. In this regard, there is a kind of vulnerability within them in a certain area. Sometimes, the term, *pain points* is used regarding this vulnerability. It is within this area, that you are serving. When we consider this fact with a sense of compassion for the person we are serving, we experience a deep respect for the other, which supports respect for ourselves.

In this respect, we think of the other the way we would want another to think of us – with our true best interest in mind. If we think of ourselves as 'selling' them something, we may want to change 'selling' to 'serving' or 'helping' because we know the benefits it will bring into their life. Then it becomes our responsibility to support them and guide them in the decision to obtain what we have to offer.

This simple change in perspective creates a new calm and empowering change within us, as we move from a self-serving, fear-based, weaker perspective to an other-serving, compassion-based, stronger perspective.

Goal-Setting
- Key Module 4 -

***With my goal-setting practice,
I am the writer of my story,
the author of my destiny.***

In a few years, when you look back on your career or professional life, you will see that it involved a story, a very personal story about a key area of your life – your purpose. You will realize that you were the writer, director, and the main character of the story. Will it feel that way, or will it feel like someone else wrote it or directed it?

In this module, you prepare for the answer that it was *you* who wrote and directed your story. And so, Keyholder Meditation for Entrepreneurs places you in the role of the writer of your story. Then when you look back, whether next week, next year, or three years from now, you will see that it was, and is, truly *your* story.

Your story begins with your Statement of Purpose, as follows:

"I am helping people who _____ by _____."

With your statement of purpose, you develop goals regarding what you want to see happening *through* your purpose. And then, you begin your planning to achieve your goals. In this way, your statement of purpose is like the title of your story, and you become the writer of your own story, and the author of your own destiny.

Goal-Setting
- Key Module 5 -

In my present moment reality,
I am using my intuition and meditation
to discover goals that my future should hold.

What exactly is goal-setting? Let's dive into this fascinating topic with an observation about reality. We live in a *physical* reality filled with people, places, things that bring joy and pain, rewards and challenges, and opportunities to explore realms of personal experience.

We also live in a *mental* reality. In this reality, when you look behind you, the view contains the actual events of your past. When you look in front of you, your view contains the imagined events of your future.

And here in the present moment, you stand between the two, between the realm of memory and the realm of imagination. It is here that you bring your intelligence and intuition to transform experiences of your past and intuitive knowledge into goals for your future.

In every moment, you are maintaining the sense of what you know and a future that is unknown. And you stand between the two, in the transcendent present moment. And as one who meditates, you can more easily access the present moment to intuitively discover what your future should hold. And so, the message of this module is to use your practice of meditation to *discover* events (goals) that exist in your future as part of your person destiny.

Goal-Setting
- Key Module 6 -

I am a student of life.
When I achieve some goals
and don't achieve others,
both experiences teach me valuable lessons.

Goal-setting can produce a subtle kind of stress. Goals can make people feel impatient. Not achieving one's goals can make a person feel unworthy, unhappy, etc.
Since meditation is about experiencing a state of calm clarity, the Keyholder system is designed to support calm.

So, let's begin with a working Keyholder definition of a goal that removes any negative stress that we might attach to it. And the definition is: *A goal is an opportunity to have certain experiences.* These experiences can produce enjoyment and/or learning.

Considering that some goals are realized, and some are not, our definition can produce a positive result in either scenario. If the goal is realized, there is a natural satisfaction that comes from the feeling of achievement. If the goal is not realized, we may still have an experience that we enjoy, and certainly we can learn from it. If we continually miss our goals, it can be a message that we might want to change our planning (which we will explore in our next topic). Or it may mean that we want to change the types of goals that we are setting, until we reach an acceptable number of achieved goals.

Goal-Setting
- Key Module 7 -

To stay in touch with my personal destiny,
I am writing down my probability goals,
higher possibility goals, and transformative goals,
and reflecting on them.

We are writing a story that connects our past and future.

- And so, we have events that we believe will definitely happen (simple to-do list action items).
- We have events that will probably happen (goals that should be achieved based on our history of reaching such goals).
- Then we have higher goals that possibly may happen (goals that involve transitions into new areas or levels of performance and productivity).
- And then there are those transformative goals (goals which when reached will positively change the way we fundamentally view ourselves).

When we write down our probability goals, higher possibility goals, and transformative goals, we find that the process is very interesting, engaging, empowering, settling, steadying, and very personal. So, begin in the spirit of the writer who is working within the reality of the blank page and its freedom, rather than the reality of the outer world and its constraints. And naturally, this approach involves practicing Meditation and using its calm, clear and intuitive state to discover your items, and recording them in your Keynotes.

Planning
- Key Module 8

*My goals, objectives, and action items
are the events, plot points, and plot of my story.
And I'm the main character –
a role I am freely choosing
and stepping into every day.*

Once we choose a goal, we begin planning on how we will achieve our goal. The first thing we can do is to apply critical path objectives to support the goal. These are the things that must happen if the goal is to be achieved. Using an online instructor as an example: If the instructor wants to secure a certain number of students, the critical path might include securing an online meeting site, finding prospective students, presenting services to the prospects, handling the transactions, meeting them at the site, and providing them the lessons.

Continuing with the spirit of the writer, if your goal is thought of as an event within an act in your play, or a scene in your movie or TV series, then these critical path objectives are plot points. And finally, there are the action items that support the objectives. In the writer's metaphor, these items make up the plot of your story.

Once you have your goal, objectives, action items (events, plot points, and plot) established, the next step is for you to enter the role, become the character, and act the part defined by your story. So, enjoy yourself and see what you experience and learn along the way.

Planning
- Key Module 9

*I am recalling excellent moments from my past
to plan excellent moments in my future.*

Meditating on the process of planning can produce intuitive strategies. For example, an online instructor or author might secure an endorsement from a high achiever in the area that they are teaching. At the multinational corporate level, a strategy that emerges in an idea mining or brainstorming session might be to develop a deeper, intuitive understanding of emerging technologies and adapting them to the corporation's plans.

Planning is about developing and implementing advanced ideas to fulfill your purpose and vision. In a meditative life, this involves using higher intelligence or intuition to find the ideas. Since you are already engaging in meditation, it will be easier for you to engage in this process.

In our system, along with looking to the future, we will also be looking to the past. Your past is a storehouse of extraordinary events and experiences that reveal how you have achieved goals. The idea is to let these events and experiences emerge while meditating, stimulate your thinking for plans, and record them in your Keynotes. Then you can test them in your operations and bring the results back into your meditation to create an upward spiral of forward movement and progress.

Planning
- Key Module 10

By recording my plans in my Keynotes,
I am creating my own practical guidebook
for my own personal success in my purpose.

One way to plan your future by accessing your past is to begin with a word like 'excellence' or phrases like 'my best performance' or 'my defining moments' and wait for memories to rise to the surface. Record them in bullet points or more elaborated if you prefer. This will be your strategic planning go-to resource that contains past content to imagine your future possibilities and design your plans for realizing them.

The moment you write your first entry, you will sense the power of the process. Look at your entry and think of a possibility that it suggests in reaching a goal and write it below or next to it. In this way, your future becomes a natural extension of your most excellent past. And since you are drawing from your most excellent experiences, you will be defining your finest and most excellent future.

The next phase engages your imagination. And this involves meditating and letting your mind be free to envision the ultimate possibilities that can derive from the excellent experiences and events that you have recorded.

As you record your plans and ideas in your Keynotes, you are writing your own personal guidebook for success.

Organization
- Key Module 11 -

Organization plays a significant role in my success.
So, I constantly work on improving
my organization skills.

Organization in your entrepreneurial life can include how your workspace is organized, how your data is organized, how people are organized. It can involve how a website, social media, communications are organized. It can encompass functions and roles, formal and informal leadership designations.

As soon as you begin organizing, you realize how effective organization can create an ease of access of people, places, things, and information. Good organization supports easy movement through well-defined pathways, serving various functions.

Organization is all about keeping things in proper order. For any purposeful endeavor, organization plays a significant role in helping you achieve your goals. Implementing effective organizational structures will help you personally and professionally and will be reflected in the completion of your everyday responsibilities.

In these ways, organization provides a sense of control and supports increased productivity.

Organization
- Key Module 12 -

I am using my organization skills to support my planning, my goals, and my positive results.

Organization and Goals. Developing your longer-range goals will make it easier to define your shorter-range goals. Think about what you want to happen in three years, then work back, defining what needs to happen to support it. Once you can see the progression from your present moment to your long-range goal, prioritize what is most important for you to do in the immediate days and weeks ahead. Look at what you have defined and organize to support it.

Organization and Planning. Be sure that your organizing follows your planning. Roles, relationships, expectations, and functions that your strategic planning require should fit into your vision, plans, goals, objectives, action items as well as your evaluation system to create organizational structures that best support your purpose.

Organization and Success. Be sure that your organizing focuses on results. When results are not achieved, purpose is not supported, and people are not served. Be sure your organizing supports action and outcomes over reflection and insights. Whereas introspection and analysis are important, involvement and achievement are vital if your purpose is to help others. Organize with this in mind.

Organization
- Key Module 13 -

I am using my organization skills to organize my workspace, develop needed skills, and lead my company.

Organizing Space and Information. Reflect on your purpose and look at how you can organize your workspace in a way that most serves your activities and goals. Look at how you organize information into projects and reports, people into groups, appointments, meetings.

Organization and Skills. Be sure that skills match goals. An efficient and effective organization requires that the skills are there to perform its required tasks. This is such a simple and basic truth, yet it is often overlooked. Demystify the process of success by realizing that it is simply about having the right skills to perform the right activities to achieve the goals that support your purpose of helping others. Look objectively at what is needed to achieve your goals and then look objectively at yourself and those who are part of your organization. Determine whether you and/or they possess the required skills?

Organization and Leadership. See all the components of your organization as parts of a whole that is wholly about serving others through your purpose. Define, establish, and maintain organizational structures in a way that allow for the natural channeling of your leadership into your purpose.

Organization
- Key Module 14 -

*I am adjusting my organization as needed
based on the everyday realities
of my company and brand.*

Organization and Day-to-Day Realities. Be sure to watch the daily running of your company or brand. Learn from what is happening in the everyday routines. Instead of having inflexible rules regarding how to achieve your goals, pay close attention to what actually happens in the day-to-day actions, interactions, and outcomes, and let them guide you in modifying your organization as needed.

Sometimes, more insight and wisdom can be obtained thinking on your feet than sitting in a chair.

Whether it's about keeping an eye on your technology, your communications, your strategic planning, skill development for yourself or your team, or having productive meetings, applying your organization skills to these everyday areas within your brand or company will produce more personal satisfaction, empowerment and enjoyment for you and your team, along with a sense of inner calm clarity that will support optimal performance and productivity.

Time-Management
- Key Module 15 -

*I am managing my time
to create those timeless experiences referred to as
being in the moment, being in the 'here and now'
being in the flow of life, or being in the zone.*

We have invented the concept of Time through the observation of a natural system. Human time is essentially based on the position of the sun, the moon, the stars, the change in the seasons. Time is utilitarian. If Time doesn't actually exist, as our latest science suggests, we have created the useful illusion of it. And now we have seconds, minutes, hours, days, months, and years. And we have insurance tables, mortgages, investment futures, transportation timetables, telecommunications scheduling. Time is simply a fact of human life, and a useful tool for your purpose, if used effectively

The meditative state involves a sense of being in the 'here and now'. There is a timeless feeling within this quality. Although this inner experience carries a timeless quality; your goals exist in time. And here is the connection:

Effective time-management will support your ability to let go of the worries about time and give yourself totally to the moments within your scheduled activities. This supports the experience of the here and now present moment, and that timeless quality that is representative of our higher nature.

Time-Management
- Key Module 16 –

*I am practicing effective time-management
to achieve my goals,
to get in touch with how time works,
and to discover what is most essential to my success.*

Time-management is a tool by which we achieve our goals within a planned timeframe. As our goals represent our individual personal natures, managing time is a way to affirm and respect ourselves.

Time-management gets us in touch with the realities of Time in the outer world, how it works, and how it can expand or contract based on the quality of our energy, our actions, and our effort.

Time-management teaches us how to imagine an event or outcome and make it happen in a year, a month, a week, or a day.

Time-management hones our thinking regarding what is essential to our purpose and our intention of helping others. We only have a certain amount of time. If we split our focus between what is essential and what is not, we will see the effect of our split focus on our performance and results.

Time-Management
- Key Module 17 –

*I am practicing effective time-management
to make sure there is enough time for what I want to achieve.
I am learning that I need less time to achieve
when I am healthier, when I practice meditation,
and when I can manage and reduce harmful stress.*

Time-management teaches us to appreciate time and to make sure we have enough of it for what we want to do and achieve.

Time-management makes us aware that time can be expanded or contracted by another element – our health. If we have less mental, physical, and/or emotional energy, we may need more time to achieve. If we have more, we may require less time. This fact of life inspires us to watch our health, fitness, nutrition, rest, and sleep habits.

Time-management reveals how meditation can store and restore energy within us to give us more time. There is a widely accepted theory that 20 minutes of deep meditation can equal two hours of sleep.

Time can cause stress, and effective time-management can reduce stress. When you take on more than you can handle, it can result in stress, strain, or burnout. When you feel in control of your situation and the time aspects of your situation, it can result in a calmer, more peaceful and healthier state.

Time-Management
- Key Module 18 –

*I am practicing effective time-management
and seeing how it supports my personal nature,
creates a healthy balance in my life,
and gives me the power to control my future.*

Time-management can create a calm and powerful sense of steadiness and rhythm in your life by supporting your personal patterns of activity within your chosen timeframes. *Search 'biorhythm and productivity' to dive into this idea.*

Time-management allows you to look at the different areas of your life and devote the amount of energy you want to spend on each of them, supporting a healthy balance.

Time-management helps you to see, predict and control the future. The future is a feature of Time. It exists conceptually because we have created seconds, minutes, hours, days, weeks, months, and years, and we can imagine them laid out ahead of us. It is a precious item in our lives to be treated with great care and respect.

When we mentally travel into the future with the intention of shaping it, we should do so with the recognition that we are being creators – creators of reality. This point of view can reduce and remove the nonessential, the unimportant, and the potentially negative elements from our character and our actions.

Skill Development
- Key Module 19 -

I am learning to develop needed skills
by actually doing the activities
for which I need the skills.

What is a skill? A skill is the ability to achieve something, to produce something, to complete something, to affect something, to influence someone.

A skill is the ability to do something.

How do we develop skills? The Keyholder answer is:

You develop a skill by doing the thing
that you want to develop the skill to do.

If this answer sounds like a riddle, it is.

And the solution to the riddle is that a skill is developed after the fact, not before the fact. Yes, you can read. You can study. You can train. You can program yourself. But the ultimate real-world skill does not develop until the action is performed and the real-world result is achieved.

Then you can assess the degree to which, and the quality at which you can perform the skill.

Skill Development
- Key Module 20 -

*I realize that I have a skill
after I succeed and have the result
for which I am practicing the skill.*

Imagine you are on a campaign to sell 10,000 items. The item sells for $20. It is sold online. You know some facts about your customer. You know the function your product serves in a particular area of your customer's life. You have found some ideas about selling, some ideas about online selling, some ideas about your brand culture. This is all well and good. But there is not yet a relevant skill developed in this picture. The skill occurs when you present your product or service for sale. Then you have a result that tells you your level of skill. And then you have some factual knowledge on which to begin further developing your skills.

Once you have a result to observe and assess, you realize that you were the cause of a particular effect. You realize it was you who created this effect, and that it had an impact within a particular environment or field. When acting and interacting in this way, we can refer to it as engaging in a creative field.

In other words, the environment that includes the customer, the product, the online media, and all aspects involved in the campaign is a field that exists for you to develop your creativity – your ability to *create* something.

Skill Development
- Key Module 21 -

*When I achieve a result with a particular skill,
I am in my element, and creating something
that can move from a possibility
to a probability to an actuality,
and finally, to a new reality.*

When you develop a skill and achieve a result with your skill, the thing you create can exist in one of four levels or stages – a possibility, probability, actuality, and finally a reality.
In a sales scenario, the prospective customer represents a possibility. As the prospect moves toward purchase, they represent a probability. When they purchase, they represent actuality. And when they use and benefit from the product, they are in the new reality that exists within your product and brand culture.

If you are in your right element - in the creative field that is suited to you, the simple engagement will bring you natural feelings of personal satisfaction, empowerment, and enjoyment.

What does it mean to be in your right element or a creative field suited to you? You are here in this world to realize your higher purpose and actualize your inner potentialities. For this reason, you find yourself inclined toward settings, scenes, and situations that involve the development of your natural talents, skills, traits, aptitudes, inclinations, etc. These settings, scenes, and situations make up the creative field. When you are achieving your intended goals in a purpose that helps others and in a way that is personally rewarding to you, you have found the element or the creative field that is suited to you.

Skill Development
- Key Module 22 -

I am getting to know more and more about myself regarding the innate gifts of my personal talents and skills, and accepting them, expressing them, and practicing them.

As an important step in a life of purpose, become aware of your natural talents, skills, and traits. Get to know yourself and respect these innate gifts that you possess.

Whatever they are, don't judge, just accept that they are yours, and feel your natural inclination to want to express them, channel them, and practice them. Notice how your qualities and inclinations express and contribute to your individual nature and particular personality. Sense your inner higher nature as you discover, express, and practice your personal traits, qualities, and skills.

Once you truly connect to your purpose, you will discover how your inner nature is actually all about those innate talents. Then practicing skills that channel your inner nature becomes a direct expression of your inner self.

To apply this idea, you can do a deep dive: look at your life and identify skills that you have developed that feel most natural to you. List them in your Keynotes. Imagine them as items on your resume or in your bio. Then dive even deeper into who you are and discover skills you might not put on a resume but that are skills, nonetheless. The same way that you use your full attentiveness in the inner practice of meditation, use that same level of awareness and attention to understanding your inner self by looking at your obvious and not-so-obvious talents and skills that you have developed in your life.

Problem-Solving
- Key Module 23 -

*I am not placing any value on a problem,
other than it is simply something to be solved,
and I am determined to solve it.*

When a particular skill is not developed to the degree required to achieve an intended outcome, the situation might then be called a problem. The ways of discovering, exploring, and implementing a solution are then considered or discussed.

So, it could be said that entrepreneurial problem-solving represents a more complex level of engagement within a creative field. The complexity might involve confronting personal feelings about your situation, or a situation that is more involved than you imagined, or a goal that carries new challenges once it is achieved.

The word 'problem' might suggest a negative condition. Within the Keyholder system, it is more of something like a math problem, neither negative nor positive, simply something to be solved. And like math, problems have different 'fields', like trigonometry, probability, topology, and statistics.

Problem fields for the entrepreneur might include marketing, expansion, innovation, regulation, diversity, staffing, customer acquisition, etc.

Problem-Solving
- Key Module 24 –

*With my inner calm meditative focus,
I am recognizing potentially problematic situations
before they become fully problematic
and negatively impactful.*

Considering the fact that we are on a meditation journey, take a moment to remember how you feel after a good meditation session – your sense of physical ease, feeling focused, mentally clear, emotionally calm and resilient. Thoughts have subsided, movement has stopped, disturbances and distractions have been quelled.

One important goal in our purposeful life within the Keyholder approach is to bring these qualities into our life. So, let's now consider a new way to experience problems.

Consider that preceding a situation becoming problematic to your brand or company, it is moving toward becoming problematic. It is a more subtle condition or state. And because of its relative dormancy, this kind of situation can go unnoticed and turn into a full-blown problem with serious impact on your brand. With your practice of meditation, you can become more aware of such subtle states and conditions, and sense where there is potential movement toward a problem that can create a negative impact and momentum (which will then require that much more effort to stop and reverse).

Problem-Solving
- Key Module 25 –

I am grateful for problems as learning opportunities, and I'm developing an understanding and mastery for identifying the nature of problems.

So, let's think of problems as useful things, necessary things that are part of our learning process. Make an affirmation that you will not stress and worry about problems in your life, but rather you will be grateful for them as they help you identify those things that you truly want to be, do, and have in life. Adopting this attitude is very supportive to your meditative practice, as meditation is about experiencing the calm in the storm. And then, in turn, your calm meditative focus can help you to resolve problems or prevent them.

It may be useful to think about problems in different ways:

- A problem can be something that blocks our path.
- A problem can be a person who presents challenges.
- Problems can be found in our own actions, reactions and interactions that produce stress, obstacles, setbacks.
- Contextually, problems can be reoccurring or non-reoccurring.
- Problems might be unique, requiring a completely new perspective or adaptation.
- A problem might indicate another problem. (For example, an entrepreneur may want to utilize marketing affiliates, but is not sure how they feel about an ongoing brand relationship and its implications or challenges.)

Problem-Solving
- Key Module 26 -

I have a process for solving problems that involves five questions with answers coming out of the practice of meditation.

One way to solve a problem is let answers to the following questions come out of your meditative practice.

1) What is a problem related to your purpose, stated as simply as possible.

2) What do you know about the problem that can help you to better understand it and potentially resolve it?

3) What deeper information can you access regarding the problem (how you think or feel about it, environmental or cultural factors, the root of the problem, etc.)

4) What insights, potential solutions, or out-of-the-box possibilities are you discovering to solve the problem?

5) How will you implement the solution you have chosen, and measure the results?

Consider that when you have identified a problem situation and set the foundation for a solution to emerge, it may not emerge if you remain in the typical ritualistic linear mindset of the everyday world. This is where the practice of meditation can open new possibilities. With the deeper insightful thinking that develops with daily meditation, you can remain in your everyday role and function most effectively, and you can also enter a state in which extraordinary insights and revelations emerge.

Communication
- Key Module 27 -

By understanding that thoughts and words embody energy,
I can achieve a higher level of mastery
in my communication skills.

In the practice of meditation, you have the extraordinary opportunity to experience yourself as both speaker and listener. We discover this when we become aware of our thinking mind while meditating and realize that we are engaging in what is often referred to as *internal dialog*. We silently speak words and we simultaneously listen to the words we are speaking.

While meditating, we can blend this commonplace dual process with the meditative qualities of awareness, patience, and equanimity, which prepares us to become extraordinary communicators and enjoy the benefits that come with it. Consider the power in your communications if you can speak and listen with full awareness, patience and equanimity.

Regarding speaking and listening, a Keyholder explanation of communication is found in these two definitions:

Speaking is the transmission or projection of an energy-embodied thought to another or others.

Listening is the receiving or reception of an energy-embodied thought from another or others.

Communication
- Key Module 28 -

I appreciate the extraordinary power that comes with listening to someone with no outer distractions, and no distractions from my own thoughts, interpretations, etc.

Since everything is essentially energy, every thought carries its own energy. When a thought is articulated through verbal language, it takes the form of a word. So, when a word is spoken, it holds both its definition and its energy. The definition is what allows us to mentally comprehend its meaning, and its energy allows us to understand the emotion or motivation of the one who used it.

If we listen within a purely receptive state to our own thoughts, we will learn truths about ourselves that we might not often reveal to others. If we listen to others in the same state of receptivity, we may find our relationships, our state of mind, our general social effectiveness, our purpose in life, our entrepreneurial journey, and our general well-being all improving.

The reason that listening in this manner can be difficult is that we are so often distracted by our own thoughts. It's like trying to listen to two people talking at the same time. Think of the power we can experience if we just listen to another to truly receive and understand what they are saying ... and feeling!

Communication
- Key Module 29 -

I am aware of different kinds of energy embodied in people's thoughts and words; and this awareness is making me a more empathic and effective communicator.

What kinds of energy do we find embodied in people's thoughts? What intention or motivation produces a thought that then transmits through the spoken or written language? In our Keyholder system, we will use a model of seven kinds of energy.

1. Foundation motivations, such as feeling safe and secure, connected, supported, trusting.

2. Creative motivations, such as feeling spontaneous, passionate, outgoing, confident, open and kind.

3. Personality motivations, such as feeling self-esteem, self-respect, a sense of individuality, personal power, and assertiveness.

4. Love-based motivations, such as compassion, acceptance, trust, inspiration, and empathy.

5. Self-expression based motivations, such as honesty, truthfulness, sincerity, authenticity, and transparency.

6. Intuitive based motivations, such as found in wisdom, insight, revelation, transcendence, and high intelligence.

7. Awareness based motivations, such as feelings of calm power, inner personal value, knowledge beyond the ego and linear thinking, and connection with all things.

Communication
- Key Module 30 –

I am communicating with the intention of supporting the person or people with whom I am communicating, and to improve and enhance our relationship.

Positive qualities of the energies embodied in one's thoughts and words can include safety, security, connectedness, trust, creativity, self-esteem, love, honesty, sincerity, and wisdom. If such positive qualities are missing or if a person feels in need of the related qualities, the person can become negatively affected. Optimally, we share the good feelings of positively motivated people; and provide support, inspiration, encouragement, etc. to the negatively affected.

When we listen to also understand motivations and feelings, we learn how to communicate with people in a way that stimulates thoughts, feelings, and actions. Obviously, this is important when we are in a purpose that involves marketing, sales, or any form of influential communication, such as teaching, counseling, the creative and performing arts, etc.

The insight here is that by letting ourselves be influenced by others, we learn to influence others. In other words, the quality of our listening skill can directly determine our speaking effectiveness. When we speak and listen in this way within the reference of our purpose, we become extraordinarily focused. Our communications become clear, concise, and efficient.

Communication
- Key Module 31 –

*I am applying my spoken word communication skills
to the written word and other forms of media.
And with these skills, I am supporting my purpose
of helping others with my brand.*

When we gain mastery with the spoken word, we can then apply it to the written word - in other words, applying our in-person experience to other media. In this way, we become proficient at communicating in various formats and on diverse platforms. With this enhanced ability to communicate within our purpose, we become more skilled at communicating in areas that support a successful project, campaign, etc.

So, a key activity to support effective communication is to listen to receive both the meaning of the words as well as the emotions and/or motivations within them, and to speak in a way that clearly, concisely, and effectively expresses the message and feeling you are intending.

You can practice and prepare for this while meditating when you pay attention (listen) to a thought that emerges (is internally spoken) and discover your feeling or motivation within the thought – with the realization that you can then bring this skill into your interactions with others to develop and strengthen your intuitive and excellent communication skills.

Self-Presentation
- Key Module 32 -

*I am committed to helping others with my purpose, and with my commitment, I am fully present in my life.
By being authentically present,
I present myself authentically.*

A Keyholder definition of Self-Presentation is the natural and positive expression of who you are through your words, mannerisms, actions, general demeanor and personal style.

So, who are you?

In reference to your meditative practice, you are an inner self - an intuitive being that exists within the context of all the content of your life. The meditation-entrepreneurship connection here is that when you are feeling most natural in your purpose, you can be fully present in each moment of life.

> You can be fully 'present',
> as in 'presentation',
> as in' 'self-presentation'.

When you are fully present, you are aware of your 'self' as a recognized fixed point within your being, so you are no longer worried or second-guessing yourself. You are comfortable with yourself, which results in a relaxed, confident, and friendly demeanor. You carry yourself effortlessly and remain poised in diverse situations.

Self-Presentation
- Key Module 33 –

*Being fully present, and presenting myself authentically,
I am more naturally poised, and associate with others
who share a natural and positive sense of self.*

When you are fully present, you are so clear about yourself that you become less concerned with yourself and more interested in other people. This gives you a heightened social effectiveness along with heightened feelings of personal satisfaction and enjoyment when in the company of others.

With each action, interaction, and reaction in which you are clear about yourself and remain poised, you become even *more* clear about yourself and poised. There is a natural cumulative process that makes life even more satisfying, empowering, and enjoyable. This results in a feeling of looking forward to each new moment. We can call the process of developing this clarity and poise, 'clearing the air', with 'air' being an acronym for actions, interactions and reactions.

When you live with this kind of personal clarity and poise, you tend to find others who share your natural sense of self and begin associating with people who have found their way to a higher, inner, deeper meaning of success in their life. In this way, you develop a support system based on higher values, since people who are self-actualized tend to be more in touch with their higher natures.

Self-Presentation
- Key Module 34 -

Being fully present, and presenting myself authentically, I am becoming more naturally stoic, insightful, and comprehensive in my thinking.

Present moment awareness and living, along with your authentic self-presentation reduces distracting thoughts of self-doubt and the uncertainty and indecisiveness that comes with it. So, your mind is free, and you become more insightful and intuitive.

You can more easily see the big picture, since you are no longer preoccupied with the minutia of worrying about yourself. You think higher thoughts, find new, innovative, out-of-the-box approaches in all areas of your life, with your entrepreneurship improving in surprising ways.

You realize that your values represent your strengths, and you focus on them. This naturally opens doors to where you can practice your strengths. And this produces positive outcomes, which in turn opens doors to greater and ever-expanding opportunities.

Since you are so clear on who you are, you no longer take things personally, but rather how they reflect the person that is expressing them. Things no longer stick to you, requiring further introspective work to release you from them. You are becoming more and more free, and it shows in your authentic self-presentation.

Self-Presentation
- Key Module 35 -

*Being fully present,
and presenting myself authentically
brings a number of benefits into my life.*

Features and benefits of authentic self-presentation include:

- Your physical demeanor - the way you move and carry yourself - changes to reflect your sense of calm powerful confidence.
- Your speaking tone and style become more natural and relaxed.
- You dress in a way that reflects the real you and your purpose, whatever it happens to be (i.e., classic, artsy, corporate, chic, sophisticated, preppy, traditional, sporty, etc.)
- You have a positive energy that is contagious.
- You own your look, your manner, your personality. You are comfortable with yourself.

We often think about how we relate to others. A key activity is to meditate on how you relate to yourself. Think about yourself like you are another person. Notice how you think about yourself while in any situation, especially within your purposeful activities. Do you accept yourself? Do you like yourself? Do you feel comfortable being around *you*? Discover your own way to answer 'yes' to these questions.

Synergy
- Key Module 36 -

Synergy occurs when living beings come together for a larger good. I embrace synergy and look for ways to experience more of it in my life and purpose.

Just as you and I are individual selves, so is everyone else! We are an ocean of selves, and as such, we are all drops in the ocean. A drop from the ocean has the same nature as the ocean. When separated from the ocean, it is no longer called 'ocean'. It is called a 'drop'. We are all part of a group called humanity. We all have our human nature in common. When we are separated from the group, we are considered to be individuals. When part of a purposeful team, we are individual team *members*.

So first, let's consider that life can condition us to not easily experience synergy. Social problems and conflicts can lead us to the belief that we are all separate. It is our birthright and our destiny to move beyond this mindset and experience a true sense of togetherness.

This is where committing to a purpose that helps others becomes so valuable. Being part of a company, a team, a brand that is founded on the true intention of making the world a better place is a way to access the humanity within us – the ocean of positive energy that we all share. This is a vital point. It is our experience of synergy, of being part of others, that gives us access to our higher inner energy nature that connects us to all humanity.

Synergy
- Key Module 37 -

*I am bringing the power of synergy into my purpose
by seeing and evaluating people in relation to how
they can support my purpose of helping others
and making the world a better place.*

Purpose is a powerful force that supports Synergy. To access this force, be clear on your purpose and work on your commitment to your purpose and how it is making the world a better place. This will allow you to better understand others' commitment to their part of your purpose. The more you align to purpose, the deeper your experience of synergy can be.

Your purpose and your synergy regarding your purpose allows you to see and evaluate *everyone* very clearly in relation to how they can support your purpose of helping others and making the world a better place.

No matter how we have lived our lives, we are always able to experience purposeful synergy. It is never too late. We may not have had the right purpose in our past, or the right company or brand, or been in the right stage of our development to grasp its value and importance. If this is the case for you, by letting go of certain aspects of your past, you can then let in the power and energy of each present moment lived within the commitment to your purpose and the experience of purposeful synergy.

Synergy
- Key Module 38 -

***I believe in the power of synergy,
so I am always watching for ways
to bring people together
in the spirit of my brand's values.***

With synergy, we care about others and feel connected. The more we desire only for ourselves, the more disconnected we feel from the group, and subsequently disconnected to our own higher nature, since our higher nature is based on our sense of connectedness.

> The power of synergy is that it changes $1 + 1 = 2$ to $1 + 1 =$ unlimited possibilities derived from shared and coordinated activity.

So, value every single connection you make, as every connection also represents the very *idea* of connection. Each person you know opens you to knowing that many more. Enjoy the process. Enjoy your networking. Enjoy the feeling that more and more people are sharing your values, and you are sharing theirs. Such synergy is a freeing experience.

Create synergy by initiating meetings, groups, forums, platforms, even social getaways, anything that brings people together in a friendly cooperative and collaborative spirit. Look for opportunities to connect and to create conditions and contexts for connecting. See opportunities everywhere.

Synergy
- Key Module 39 -

I am learning how to bring different kinds of people together into my purpose of helping others.

Synergy can involve people who have different traits, qualities, talents and skills coming together. So, part of the process of entrepreneurial synergy is learning how to bring different kinds of people together into a common purpose that helps others.

Powerful individuals are great. But powerful groups are better. For example, consider the following equations:

- A mastermind group or a leadership team = collective intelligence = expanded benefits for you, your purpose, and the people you are supporting you through your purpose.

- Creativity + Synergy = Excellence: Creative skills, such as decision-making, problem-solving, critical thinking, etc. skills *combined with* the synergy of interpersonal, teambuilding, and communication skills can produce extraordinary results.

Open the door between yourself and another or others by sharing who you are, your life, your experiences, your personal challenges, because these specifics are actually general to all people. Therefore, when you share yourself with others, others will share themselves with you.

Leadership
- Key Module 40 -

*As a leader, my higher, inner, deeper purpose
is to support my team in experiencing
positivity and optimization in their own lives
while they are also creating it for others.*

As entrepreneurs who meditate, our journey is an inner journey. And so, in our system of Keyholder Meditation, we translate commonplace concepts into deeper ideas, using metaphors in the process. In this way, we arrive at the heart of a matter, at the inspired intention that produces results of the highest kind.

We use a metaphor in the Synergy modules with the ocean referring to the collective, and a drop in the ocean, the individual. So, synergy is experienced as being the ocean within the drop, the group's purpose being embodied in the group member.

Amidst all the synergy is a drop that firmly knows that they are the ocean – in the service of guiding and supporting others to experience their own synergistic unique individuality. This is the leader.

In Keyholder thinking, a leader presents an opportunity for people to experience their true higher, inner nature.

Leadership
- Key Module 41 -

*As an entrepreneurial leader,
I promote the experience of synergy in my team
by practicing it myself and creating conditions
and situations for it to naturally develop.*

The entrepreneurial leader sees that every challenge and problem that arises on the journey as an opportunity to strengthen commitment, along with the skills needed to solve the problem or meet the challenge.

Simply stated, the leader is in the practice of transformation. At some point, the leader shows that transformation is a change in how we experience something, a new way of seeing something. The leader brings team members from their individual experience to the heights of synergistic experience while supporting and celebrating their individuality.

Imagine a brand or a company being a person, and within that person is a higher being. In this regard, a being can be a noun, as in the word, *person*, or it can be a verb, as in *a way of existing*. As a leader, you represent this higher being. And in this manner, you become transcendent and transparent, enlivening the organization with your intuitive insight. All that you knew as 'yourself' or 'your 'ego', diminishes or disappears to reveal the pure purpose of the company or group. And this transparency supports your team to experience the full power and meaning of your brand and your purpose of helping others.

Leadership
- Key Module 42 -

*As a positive entrepreneurial leader,
I lead with integrity and accountability,
which inspires integrity and accountability
in those I am leading.*

With your pure spirit of helping others and intention of making the world a better place, you lead from a place of integrity. Integrity means that you are perfectly integrated into the purpose of your brand or company, and your actions originate from the vision and goals derived from that purpose.

With this integrity, you create conditions for others to take action that both serves the purpose and empowers the person. The way they deepen their own integrity is by doing those things that they say they will do on behalf of the company and brand, knowing that the ultimate purpose is in the helping of others.

And you, as the leader are the one to whom the person gives their word, therefore creating a line of accountability to you. To say it more personally, they create a relationship with you built on respect and trust.

A purposeful group, organization or company is a collective accountability – from the leader to the population served, from the leader to the members of the organization, and from the organization to the leader.

Leadership
- Key Module 43 -

*As a positive entrepreneurial leader,
I take action and inspire my team to take action.
And the purposeful action we all take is performed
in the spirit of helping others.*

The way that the leader creates new possibilities for the future of their brand or company is by taking action and directing the team's members to take action. Then data is gathered based on the outcomes of *the actions*. Purpose, vision, setting goals, and planning are important, but it is action that grows a company and a brand. The customers respond to action. The world responds to action. It is action that spurs customers and the world to action. So, leadership becomes more than the concept or idea of *being a leader* once you are already leading.

The reality of leadership is in the action you take and direct, not in your title. And your action results in the answers to two questions: 'Who is being helped?' 'How are they being helped?' As leader, you keep questioning on these two points, and you question about everything! When someone says something, you keep questioning! When you receive data, you keep questioning.

Asking questions to obtain information, taking action, and directing action to support the mission of one's purpose and brand. These are the hallmarks of the caring leader.

Positivity
- Key Module 44 -

*I am a positive person, and as an entrepreneur,
my intention is to create positivity and optimization for
myself and for others through my purpose and my brand.*

The practice of Keyholder Meditation for Entrepreneurs is meant to support you in setting the foundation for a positive life. And a positive life involves being in, or moving toward an optimal state, optimizing a situation, optimizing health, etc.

If we don't take positive action to optimize, the opposite will occur by default. That is, our life will move toward *entropy*, which is a state of disorder, uncertainty and unpredictability that can ultimately lead to chaos and destruction.

In your life as a compassionate, purpose-centered entrepreneur, a positive perspective begins with the spirit of helping others – a clearly positive value to hold and express.

And with this value supporting your purpose and the practice of meditation, you align the entrepreneurial skills of goal setting, planning, organization, time management, and so on, until you arrive at this 12th and final area of the Keyholder Meditation for Entrepreneurs practice, where you formally recognize yourself and your intentions as being positive, and yourself as representing a positive force in our world.

Positivity
- Key Module 45 -

*I am adopting a positive systems approach,
and learning to see all that I do as it relates
to positivity and optimization.*

From a single atom to the entire universe itself, everything is a system. Everything is a process that involves an interplay. The parts of the process are in relationship with each other, and the relationships form the character of the process that creates certain outcomes. When you adopt positivity as the basis of your system, you see all of the entrepreneurial qualities and skills as they support positivity and optimization.

A positive systems approach integrates and aligns all the components and aspects of your purpose to the motivation of helping others. With this approach, you can then understand and experience all parts in relationship to your positive and optimizing perspective.

A systems approach permits you to illuminate strengths and weaknesses, and the driving and restraining forces acting upon the system both internally and externally. With a systems approach, you can more easily recognize opportunities, as well as anything that can potentially threaten the integrity and success of the system. Simply stated, it reveals valuable information and insights to support your purpose.

And finally, regarding the meditation connection, the most effective mind state supporting a positive systems approach is one that blends the intuitive and rational. And a most efficient process for accessing this mind state is found in the practice of meditation.

Positivity
- Key Module 46 -

I am supporting my positive life as an entrepreneur by practicing meditation for its positive benefits, including how it can support my spirit of helping others and my goal-setting and planning.

As an entrepreneur who practices meditation, you have the advantage of using your inner practice to access intuitive knowledge and insights to support your brand, your company, and your purpose.

For example, you can use your meditation practice to intuitively define how you are **helping others** with your purpose: how you are bringing positive change into the lives of the people you are helping, how you are helping them to optimize their life related to the function, features and benefits of your product, service or content.

Having defined your purpose and how it helps others, you can then use your meditation practice to reveal significant **goals** that will support your brand and advance your purpose.

And then, with your purpose and significant goals defined, you can use your meditative practice to access your intuitive thinking, discover insights to make **plans** for the future of your brand, your company, and your purpose.

Positivity
- Key Module 47 -

I am supporting my positive life as an entrepreneur by practicing meditation for its positive benefits, including how it can support my organization, time-management, skill-development, problem-solving, and communication.

As an entrepreneur who practices meditation, you have the advantage of using your inner practice to access intuitive knowledge and insights to support your brand, your company, and your purpose. For example, you can define an area, such as workspace, people, process, information, etc. and use your meditative practice to gain insights regarding what is required to **organize** the area to best support your system.

You can use your meditative practice to gain insights regarding how to **manage your time** - how goals should be selected, sequenced, clustered, prioritized and monitored to best support your purpose. You can also use your meditative practice to gain insights regarding the **development of skills** that are required to support your goals.

Within the inner calm clear powerful state of your meditative practice, you can sense your system as an efficiently flowing process, and problems as ripples or blockages in the flow. Let your intuitive mind reveal ways to correct or **solve problems** and bring your system to optimal flow and efficiency.

A purpose can be viewed as a collection of communications. You can use your meditative practice to gain insights on how to improve the effectiveness and efficiency of individual and/or team **communication skills** within your system.

Positivity
- Key Module 48 -

I am supporting my positive life as an entrepreneur by practicing meditation for its positive benefits, including how it can support my self-presentation, synergy, and leadership skills to create positivity and optimization.

As an entrepreneur who practices meditation, you have the advantage of using your inner practice to access intuitive knowledge and insights to support your brand, your company, and your purpose.

For example, you can use your meditative practice to gain insights regarding elements of your **self-presentation** and style to best support your mission and brand message.

You can use your meditative practice to gain insights regarding the people involved in your purpose, their actions and interactions, their personal characters and professional roles, their individual and collective function as team members and teams. Considering these elements, let insights come to you regarding how to create and build team **synergy** to best serve your purpose of helping others.

You can also use your meditative practice to discover, define, modify, affirm or reinforce the **leadership** traits, skills and practices required to support the integrity and success of your system. Let insights come regarding who you are as a leader, and what you can do to continue growing as a compassionate, purpose-centered entrepreneurial leader.

The Eternal Clock

NAME

Imagine an eternal clock hanging on your wall with each number representing an area that supports the inner journey of the entrepreneur. Twelve *eternal* traits and skills of the successful entrepreneur is where the name derives.

FRAME

The frame of *The Eternal Clock* is that of a dice game in which the 36 possible dice rolls of two dice lead to an area of entrepreneurship, with each area featuring three questions. The game play involves: 1) rolling a pair of dice, (or using an online dice roll randomizer), 2) looking up the roll, starting on page 113, and 3) answering any or all of the questions.

AIM

The aim of *The Eternal Clock* is to support you in developing mastery in 12 important areas in the inner journey of the entrepreneur. Of course, the game can be played solo, with friends, family, associates, partners, or anyone interested in an entrepreneurial game that supports you or all who are playing.

The 'Set' of 108 Key Questions

With 36 dice roll possibilities, and each including three questions, there are 108 Key Questions in all. This 'set of questions' can be seen as a system in the way that the basic Tai Chi set of 108 movements represents a system.

You can search *'the significance of 108'* to discover or review how profound the number 108 is, and its importance in various subjects such as mathematics, astronomy, physics, sports, space flight, gaming, etc. One culture refers to 108 as the number of the wholeness of existence.

The Sequential Course/Syllabus Option

The *Keyholder Meditation for Entrepreneurs* practice can be used as a sequential course or syllabus by going go through the 48 Key Modules in the order presented, so you can opt to answer the 108 questions in sequence and follow its natural developmental progression.

And as with the Meditation practice and its 12 *modules*, you can browse through the 108 *questions* to select ones that are most important for you to explore and answer at the moment.

And of course, as with any educational course or syllabus that prepares you for success in life, you can keep notes to derive the optimal benefits for your entrepreneurial development.

The Year of the Entrepreneur

NAME

The Year of the Entrepreneur is a game activity that references the 12 Key Areas of Entrepreneurship and connects notable people with the 12 months of the year.

FRAME

The frame of *The Year of the Entrepreneur* involves thinking of a person, and discovering their birthday by asking a digital assistant or doing a quick internet search. You can also think of someone whose birthday you already know. Once you have a name and a birthday, the play involves giving a brief presentation on a notable occurrence or achievement about the person, and how it represents one of the 12 Key Areas of Entrepreneurship. The Key Area is determined by the birth month number. 1 for January, 2 for February, through to 12 for December.

MONTH	#	AREA	MODULES
JAN	1	Helping Others	1-2-3
FEB	2	Goal-Setting	4-5-6-7
MAR	3	Planning	8-9-10
APR	4	Organization	11-12-13-14
MAY	5	Time-Management	14-15-16-17-18
JUN	6	Skill-Development	19-20-21-22
JUL	7	Problem-Solving	23-24-25-26
AUG	8	Communication	27-28-29-30-31
SEP	9	Self-Presentation	32-33-34-35
OCT	10	Synergy	36-37-38-39
NOV	11	Leadership	40-41-42-43
DEC	12	Positivity	44-45-46-47-48

Here is a list of examples of commonly known people:

Internet people and personalities. Movie actors, directors. TV People: news, commentary, talk show, reality show, game show, drama, sitcom, soap opera, TV movies. Creative people, artistic people, musical people. Athletes, business leaders, politicians, service people. Writers (Book, magazine, newspaper, online content) Historical Figures (Any of the above, and other kinds of significant figures who lived before our time).

You can also randomly select people with an internet search. Choose a category or simply use 'people' as your category. For example: Famous people. Important people. Influential people. Celebrities. You can add a number to your search. 100, 200, 1,000 famous people, etc. And you can add a category: 1,000 celebrities. 1,000 actors. 100 scientists. 100 athletes. 100 writers. 100 business leaders. 100 artists, rappers, etc.

Here are questions correlating to the 12 Key Areas:
1. How did they help others?
2. What great goal did they set and achieve?
3. How did they plan out a campaign or an achievement?
4. What did they organize?
5. What did they manage over a long period of time?
6. What great talent or skill are they known for having?
7. What problem did they solve?
8. What great speech or quote are they known for?
9. How were they known for their self-presentation?
10. How did they create synergy and team spirit?
11. What great leadership skills did they display?
12. How did they exhibit positivity and create more positive feelings in the world?

AIM

The aim of *The Year of the Entrepreneur* is to support you in the 12 Key Areas of Entrepreneurship by relating them to actual people, and exploring how the people exhibited and represented the 12 areas in their lives. We can also choose an inferred situation. For example, if you chose an actor/producer, you can infer what they would have had to do to make a particular movie so successful, related to the correlating entrepreneurial area.

This is an expansive process in that it expands our thinking about people. And this opens us to bringing more and more people into our purpose and brand culture. It also provides an engaging pastime for getting to know celebrities, famous and notable people both current and from the past. The value of this is that these are also important or successful people; and by learning about them, we feel connected to them. As we gain insight into the ways that they grew in importance, we can learn to also grow and develop our entrepreneurial status and brand.

Of course, the game can be played solo, or we can share the fun with friends, family, associates, partners, or anyone interested in an entrepreneurial game that supports you or all who are playing.

Master Key

NAME

Along with *The Year of the Entrepreneur* and *The Eternal Clock*, you can also opt to play the *Master Key* dice-game variation. The name Master Key refers to the Master Key symbol ⌐ found at the bottom of each Keyholder Meditation Module page. The numbers following the symbol are the numbers that correlate to the Key Area.

FRAME

The frame of *The Master Key Game Activity is* that of a dice game with 36 possible dice rolls. The game play involves rolling a pair of dice, (or using an online dice roll randomizer), and looking up the roll, starting on page 113. There you find and go to the Key Module pages. Then you put the Module's ideas into your own words, and create your own Intentional Key Mantra to open a door in your purpose. For example: for Synergy, you will find 36, 37, 38, 39 at the bottom of the page. So, you would browse through the Synergy Key Modules 36 through 39. And a mantra might be:

> *I will form a marketing team in which each member can earn (a certain amount), and I will foster synergy in the team to create a personally and financially rewarding experience for all involved.*

AIM

The aim of *Master Key* is to support you in developing mastery in 12 entrepreneurial areas, and relating them directly to your purpose. And of course, the game activity can be played solo or in a social setting.

THE SPIRIT OF HELPING OTHERS

- Who are the people you help with your product, service, content, or brand - who are your customers?
- What values do you have in common with them?
- How do you feel about these people?

- What success story or testimonies show how you have helped someone/others?
- What makes your customers know that you are in the true spirit of helping?
- Which of your competitors is doing a good job helping people, and what can you learn from them?

- Define your customers' needs that you are helping to fulfill with your product, service, content, or brand, and elaborate on them.
- What else do you know about your customer?
- What are the other ways that you can help them with your product, service, content, etc.?

⌬ **Master Key Modules 1, 2, 3**

GOAL-SETTING

- What are examples of goals that you have set and achieved in your life that make you positive and optimistic about your brand leadership / goal-setting abilities?
- How did you achieve them?
- What have you learned about goal-setting to support you in setting and achieving your upcoming goals?

- What method(s) do you currently use for setting goals?
- What method or methods do you currently use for monitoring and evaluating your performance and productivity regarding the goals you set?
- How can you improve on these methods?

- What is the most important transformative goal that you have in your professional life / brand leadership?
- What transformative goals do you have for your future in other areas of your life?
- How will reaching these transformative goals impact or change your life, and what are steps to achieving them?

⌱ **Master Key Modules 4, 5, 6, 7**

PLANNING

Think of a 3–6-month goal you want to achieve.
- What are steps required to achieve the goal?
- What challenges or obstacles might you find on your path to the goal?
- How can you handle the challenges, and who and what resources can help you to reach your goal?

Think of a 12–18-month goal you want to achieve.
- What are steps required to achieve the goal?
- What challenges or obstacles might you find on your path to the goal?
- How can you handle the challenges, and who and what resources can help you to reach your goal?

- Think of the longest-range goal you want to consider at this time. What are steps required to achieve the goal?
- What challenges or obstacles might you find on your path to the goal?
- How can you handle the challenges, and who and what resources can help you to reach your goal?

⌁ **Master Key Modules 8, 9, 10**

ORGANIZATION

■ What do you need in your workspace; and how do you organize your work space?

■ What kinds of information do you require; and how do you organize your information?

■ What people are involved in your purpose, and how do you organize them?

■ What digital platforms/resources are you using or planning to use?

■ How and why are you using them or planning to use them?

■ How do/can you organize your digital reality?

■ How do you (or how can you better) organize your customer information and customer communications?

■ How do you (or how can you better) organize your supply chain?

■ How are you (or how can you better) organize your financial and administrative records.

⌐ **Master Key Modules 11, 12, 13, 14**

TIME-MANAGEMENT

■ What's an example of a goal to be reached in a typical day in your current situation?

■ What's an example of a goal to be reached in a typical week in your current situation?

■ How do you manage your time to assure that you will achieve your daily and weekly goals?

■ What side project, new idea, fun activity do/can you include in your life to keep your creativity and motivation high; and how much time would you spend on it?

■ What do/can you do to relax and recharge in your day?

■ What can distract you from your purpose during your day, and how do/can you overcome the distractions?

■ What specific value and benefits does/can efficient time-management bring to you in your professional life?

■ Where can you improve in your time-management?

■ How can you bring about this improvement to realize more of the benefits of efficient time-management?

⊶ **Master Key Modules 15, 16, 17, 18**

SKILL-DEVELOPMENT

- What is the most important skill for you to develop or strengthen to grow your brand?
- What would the next priority skill be?
- How will you develop or strengthen these skills?

- What is an upcoming goal that will require that you learn something new?
- What will you have to learn?
- How can you methodically learn and develop the skills you need to develop to achieve this goal?

- What is an area of business that feels the most uncomfortable or unnatural for you regarding the skills needed in that area?
- What would have to happen to make that area feel more familiar, comfortable, and natural for you?
- How can you make it happen? How can you transition from your current state of feeling uncomfortable or unnatural to feeling natural regarding these skills?

⌛ Master Key Modules 19, 20, 21, 22

PROBLEM-SOLVING

■ What was the first problem you remember having in your life?

■ Knowing what you know now, how could you have solved that problem?

■ If you had solved that problem in this way, how would it have changed your life?

■ What problems are you facing currently that you would like to solve?

■ What are possible solutions - how do people solve typically these problems?

■ Considering your current skill set, what is the path you need to take to solve these problems?

■ What is an example of a problem that you face/faced in your life and the skill that you need/needed to handle the problem?

■ Are you solving/did you solve the problem?

■ If so, how? If not, why not?

🗝 **Master Key Modules 23, 24, 25, 26**

COMMUNICATION

- Where in your purpose is communication most important?
- How have you shown yourself to be a good communicator?
- What are important lessons you have learned about communication?

- How can you improve your communication skills?
- What kind of positive impression can you make through your communication style?
- How can you develop or strengthen your nonverbal communication skills?

- What are your strengths in digital communication?
- What digital communication skills would you like to develop or strengthen?
- How can you develop or strengthen these skills?

 ⚬⌐ **Master Key Modules 27, 28, 29, 30, 31**

SELF-PRESENTATION

■ What can you do to make people feel more comfortable being with you or being in your company?

■ What qualities do you think make a person likeable? How can you develop or strengthen these within yourself?

■ What about someone makes you trust them? How can you develop or strengthen these qualities within yourself?

■ Think of an experience that shows that the way you think about someone affects how you present yourself.

■ Think of an experience that shows that people respond to you based on how you present yourself.

■ What part of you do you not present to anyone, but wish you could? How can you present this part of you?

■ How would you describe your personal style and demeanor?

■ What, if anything, would you like to change, improve, refine, etc. regarding your personal style and demeanor?

■ How can you make such changes, improvements, refinements?

⌐ **Master Key Modules 32, 33, 34, 35**

SYNERGY

- When did you feel happy, fulfilled, effective, etc. in being part of a group or a team?
- What made your experience with that group or team a positive experience?
- How can you bring that positive kind of experience into a current team or group that you are/will be building?

- What is an example of a time when you aligned yourself to the needs of another so fully that it felt very natural to help them to fulfill their needs?
- What values did/do you share with that person? In what other ways are you similar to that person?
- How are you similar to your customers in your thoughts, feelings, interests, activities, etc.?

- How will your brand make the world a better place?
- What skills would you want represented in your perfect Mastermind group?
- Where can you find the people for your Mastermind Group, and how can you recruit them into your group?

🗝 **Master Key Modules 36, 37, 38, 39**

LEADERSHIP

■ Who has been a leadership role model in your life?
■ What did you like about their leadership style?
■ How can you develop their qualities and integrate them into your style?

■ What is a future level of success in your brand or company that requires strong leadership to achieve it?
■ How equipped are you to provide the leadership that is needed?
■ What can you do to develop or strengthen the leadership skills required to achieve that level?

■ Think of an influential person who is generally known, or an influential person you have personally known that you feel/felt is/was lacking in important leadership traits or skills?
■ How are/were they lacking? (You can share this without overtly identifying the person)
■ How can you be sure that you are not lacking in the same way?

⚿ **Master Key Modules 40, 41, 42, 43**

POSITIVITY

- What experiences or people in your past brought you positive feelings?
- What people or incidents in your past brought you negative feelings?
- What can you learn from these to bring more positive feelings into your life and less negative ones?

- What about your purpose brings you positive feelings?
- What about your purpose can potentially bring you negative feelings and experiences?
- How can you increase the positive feelings and reduce the negative ones?

- Besides the positive feelings in your purpose, at this moment in your life, what can bring positive feelings?
- Besides any possible negative feelings related to your purpose, at this moment in your life, what could bring you negative feelings?
- What can you do to increase the positive and reduce the negative in your life at this time?

⊶ **Master Key Modules 44, 45, 46, 47, 48**

Part Five
Your Brand Venture

With all that we have learned about entrepreneurship, and defined about our brand, here, in Part 5 of *Key Quest,* we are ready to dive into specific questions regarding our brand venture. As you answer the questions, you will be creating a valuable resource for your brand and your company. And as you continue traveling on your inner journey, you will be able to tap into this resource for guidance, clarity, and direction. Like a compass, it will keep your direction constant and your path clear.

Along with being a resource supporting the success of your brand, this resource will also provide you with talking points for the intelligent presentation or discussion of your purpose and your mission. (Notice that every item starts with the words, "Talk about …".) To test the quality and objectivity of your answers, imagine that the questions are coming from a team of venture capitalists that you are pitching for an investment. Since money, in the form of sales and profits, is an essential indicator of your success; money, in the form of an investment that venture capitalists are willing to make, Is an essential indicator of your potential. So, for the game version of your brand venture, we find *Keys to Adventure,* with your answers representing keys that unlock that potential.

As a developmental process here in Part 5, you will be answering the questions and recording them in your keynotes. There are 52 questions in all, organized into 13 categories, with four questions per category.

As with all the contents of this book, you can think of the list of questions as part of your own personal curriculum for your education supporting your brand's purpose and mission. Here is the list of questions, followed by the game overview, and the game, *Keys to Adventure*.

1. Overview

- Talk about your personal commitment to your purpose and brand, and how you show it.
- Talk about your spirit of helping others and compassion regarding your customers' pain points.
- Talk about your customers' testimonials and the confidence and enthusiasm they create in you.
- Talk about how speaking your truth about your purpose brings you a sense of inner calm.

2. Customers, The Market, Customer Base

- Talk about your customers' pain points, their problems for which they want to find solutions.
- Talk about your customer's journey, from when they discover your product to when they buy.
- Talk about the size of the market – the total number of potential buyers and sales.
- Talk about key characteristics of people likely to pay for your products, services, content, or brand.

3. Product

- Talk about the features and benefits of your product, service, content, or brand.
- Talk about what makes what you are offering the best on the market.
- Talk about the landed cost and price point, and any plans you have to improve on them.
- Talk about any changes you might be making to your product, or new products you can add.

4. Marketing

- Talk about how word-of-mouth works for you – why and how your customers talk you up.
- Talk about your content marketing, and how it is valuable and relevant to your customers.
- Talk about any live event marketing you have implemented, or are planning to implement.
- Talk about your email marketing, how you are using it, and what results you are having.

5. Sales

- Talk about your lifetime sales, how you have achieved them, and what they have taught you.
- Talk about your sales (or sales planning activity) in the last 12 months
- Talk about your sales (or sales planning activity) in the last three months
- Talk about your sales projections for the coming three months, twelve months, and beyond.

6. Numbers

- Talk about the cost of customer acquisition and how you plan to improve it.
- Talk about net income, cash flow, inventory, profit and loss, and your plans to improve.
- Talk about what you would do with a certain amount of money if an investor gave it to you.
- Talk about your grasp of the important numbers in your company and how you will improve them.

7. Social Media

- Talk about how you are growing (or planning to grow) an online community loyal to your brand
- Talk about engagement strategy – how you plan to have people pay attention and engage your content.
- Talk about how you are planning to drive highly targeted traffic to your website.
- Talk about how you are assuring that visitors to your website will convert, or revisit and convert.

8. Planning, Scaling

- Talk about your business plan, growth targets, and your core competency assuring success.
- Talk about the broad and complementary team skillset that is required to scale your brand.
- Talk about the collaborations and partnerships you plan to form with people and organizations to scale.
- Talk about standardized processes in place (or that you are planning) to support growth.

9. Protection, Risks, Barrier to Entry, Competition

- Talk about your brand's intellectual property, and protection such as patents or trademarks.
- Talk about your company's competitors and your brand's competitive advantage.
- Talk about barriers to entry and how they relate to your brand and your competition.
- Talk about any financial, compliance, security, or reputation risks and how you are mitigating.

10. Your Brand Story

- Talk about early stages of your brand, including creation of your MVP, beta release, and so on.
- Talk about your initial or pilot customers and any early traction in your brand story.
- Talk about when your brand became a successful brand, and the principal reasons.
- Talk about how your traction can be accelerated, and your plans for implementing your ideas.

11. Team

- Talk about how you built your team or your plans for building a team.
- Talk about the relevant domain experience and industry know-how required in your team.
- Talk about why your team (or planned team) is capable of executing your business plan.
- Talk about how having a team has, or can, impact innovation, successful adjusting, pivoting, etc.

12. Leadership/Management (1)

- Talk about your leadership skills regarding developing innovative ideas.
- Talk about your leadership skills regarding your ability to access valuable resources.
- Talk about your leadership skills on knowing your secret sauce and how to leverage it.
- Talk about the values you hold as a leader, and how these values will drive success.

13. Leadership/Management (2)

- Talk about the change you want to create in the world, and why you are the one to lead it.
- Talk about your personal traits and qualities that make you a great leader for your brand.
- Talk about how you are deepening your self-knowledge, and its impact on your success.
- Talk about a social cause you want to support with your brand, and why it is important to you.

Keys to Adventure

NAME

The name, *Keys to Adventure* refers to the adventure of the inner journey or quest. And it is also a play on words, with the word *adventure* deriving from the word *venture*, and connecting to the venture capital pitch game theme.

FRAME

The frame of the game is that of a presentation or pitch made to a venture capitalist or team of venture capitalists. The game play involves either thinking of a card, picking a card from a standard playing card deck of 52 cards, or using an online playing card randomizer, and looking up the correlating question from the Card List which is found on the four pages following this overview.

Answer the question as you would to the venture capitalists with the intention of convincing them to invest in your venture. Using a five-star scoring system, the scores would be: 1 for No, 2 for Probably Not, 3 for Maybe, 4 for Probably, and 5 for Definitely.
You can choose a number of questions for the game. The top possible score would be the total number of questions times the total number of stars received.

You can add a reality show flavor by having those in the venture capitalist roles engaging with the presenter, challenging them, etc. They can also represent various personalities. For example, the strict money-focused VC, the social cause VC, the mega-successful brand developer VC, or any personalities that you think will bring more realism and/or entertainment and fun to the game.

AIM

The aim of *Keys to Adventure* is to provide the same benefits as found in the brand venture developmental process. And like all of the Key Quest games, the game can be played solo, with friends, family members, associates, or anyone interested in an entrepreneurial game that supports you or all who are playing. And don't forget that you can use a digital assistant to define terms, explain concepts, or for general support.

The Card List is found on the following four pages.
The categories by card number and face value are as follows:

1. Overview (Ace)
2. Customers, The Market, Customer Base
3. Product
4. Marketing
5. Sales
6. Numbers
7. Social Media
8. Planning, Scaling
9. Protection, Risks, Barrier to Entry, Competition
10. Your Brand Story
11. Team (Jack)
12. Leadership/Management (Queen)
13. Leadership/Management (King)

So, think of a card or pick a card,
find your question in the Card List,
and make your pitch!

♥ KEYS TO ADVENTURE CARD LIST ♥

A♥	Talk about your personal commitment to your purpose and brand, and how you show it.
2♥	Talk about your customers' pain points, their problems for which they want to find solutions.
3♥	Talk about the features and benefits of your product, service, content, or brand.
4♥	Talk about how word-of-mouth works for you – why and how your customers talk you up.
5♥	Talk about your lifetime sales, how you have achieved them, and what they have taught you.
6♥	Talk about the cost of customer acquisition and how you plan to improve it.
7♥	Talk about how you are growing (or planning to grow) an online community loyal to your brand.
8♥	Talk about your business plan, growth targets, and your core competency assuring success.
9♥	Talk about your brand's intellectual property, and protection such as patents or trademarks.
10♥	Talk about early stages of your brand, including creation of your MVP, beta release, and so on.
J♥	Talk about how you built your team, or your plans for building a team.
Q♥	Talk about your leadership skills regarding coming up with innovative ideas.
K♥	Talk about the change you want to create in the world, and why you are the one to lead it.

♠ KEYS TO ADVENTURE CARD LIST ♠

A♠	Talk about your spirit of helping others and compassion regarding customers' pain points.
2♠	Talk about your customer's journey, from when they discover your product to when they buy.
3♠	Talk about what makes what you are offering the best on the market.
4♠	Talk about your content marketing, and how it is valuable and relevant to your customers.
5♠	Talk about your sales (or sales planning activity) in the last 12 months.
6♠	Talk about net income, cash flow, inventory, profit and loss and your plans to improve.
7♠	Talk about engagement strategy - why people will pay attention and engage your content.
8♠	Talk about the broad and complementary team skillset that is required to scale your brand.
9♠	Talk about your company's competitors and your brand's competitive advantage.
10♠	Talk about your initial or pilot customers and any early traction in your brand story.
J♠	Talk about the relevant domain experience and industry know-how required in your team.
Q♠	Talk about your leadership skills regarding your ability to access valuable resources.
K♠	Talk about your personal traits and qualities that make you a great leader for your brand.

♦ KEYS TO ADVENTURE CARD LIST ♦

A♦	Talk about your customers' testimonials and the confidence and enthusiasm they create in you.
2♦	Talk about the size of the market – the total number of potential buyers and sales.
3♦	Talk about the landed cost and price point, and any plans you have to improve on them.
4♦	Talk about your email marketing, how you are using it, and what results you are having.
5♦	Talk about your sales or sales planning activity in the last three months.
6♦	Talk about what you would do with a certain amount of money if an investor gave it to you.
7♦	Talk about how you are planning to drive highly targeted traffic to your website.
8♦	Talk about the collaborations and partnerships you plan to form with people and organizations.
9♦	Talk about barriers to entry and how they relate to your brand and your competition.
10♦	Talk about when your brand became a successful brand, and the principal reasons.
J♦	Talk about why your team (or planned team) is capable of executing your business plan.
Q♦	Talk about your leadership skills on knowing your secret sauce and how to leverage it.
K♦	Talk about how you are deepening your self-knowledge, and its impact on your success.

♣ KEYS TO ADVENTURE CARD LIST ♣

A♣	Talk about how speaking your truth about your purpose brings you a sense of inner calm.
2♣	Talk about key characteristics of people likely to pay for your products, services, or content.
3♣	Talk about any changes you might be making to your product, or new products you can add.
4♣	Talk about any live event marketing you have implemented, or are planning to implement.
5♣	Talk about your sales projections for the coming three months, twelve months, and beyond.
6♣	Talk about your grasp of the important numbers in your company and plans to improve them.
7♣	Talk about how you are assuring that visitors to your website will revisit and convert.
8♣	Talk about standardized processes in place (or that you are planning) to support growth.
9♣	Talk about any financial, compliance, security or reputation risks and how you are mitigating.
10♣	Talk about how your traction can be accelerated and your plans for implementing your ideas.
J♣	Talk about how having a team can impact innovation, successful adjusting, pivoting, etc.
Q♣	Talk about the values you hold as a leader, and how these values also will drive success.
K♣	Talk about a social cause you want to support with your brand, and why it is important to you.

Part Six
Key Points on your Journey

With our clearer understanding of our brand venture, here in Part Six, we'll develop a business plan, and learn about *Time Portal* – a game activity to further develop and refine the plan, while enjoying the play aspect. The game activity involves time travel – to six future key points of your journey: three-to-six months, nine months, one year, eighteen months, two years, and three years. Or you can spend your time and your turn staying in the present.

First, let's work on a vision. A vision motivates us. With a vision, we feel inspired and idealistic regarding our future. This supports our longer-range three-year goal. We start with three years because things change too quickly to start with anything longer than three years. So, to discover this vision, first consider your brand, your purpose, your mission, and yourself, and think about areas that should be part of your vision. These can include the following nine areas: Sales, Customers, Revenue, Staff, Support, Products, Services, Content, and Free Time for your personal interests, pastimes, leisure, etc.

Once you have a vision and three-year goals, what would you like to see happening at one year to support the longer goals? Since, your one-year goals are connected to your three-year vision, they will keep you inspired and idealistic. And since they are closer to the present, they will make you more rational and realistic regarding what you need to do to achieve them.

Now, rather than just thinking that one-year is one-third of three year and defining goals proportionately, think more about how things actually work. For example, in the area of sales, if your goal is 50,000 units sold by the end of year three, your first-year goal may be only 10,000. This is because your success should *expand* in the second year, and further in the third. So, year one might be 10,000. At year two, you might add 15,000, and total 25,000. And at year three, you might add 25,000, and total the 50,000. This progression takes into account the accumulative advantage, where results create a cumulative or domino effect with increasingly positive results and outcomes that follow the initial goal and results.

Noe, there is a natural relationship between the elements of your planning that supports the *comprehensiveness* of your business plan. For example, if a key point on your journey is to reach 10,000 *units* in sales, and this means one unit per customer, then when you achieve this goal, you will have 10,000 *customers*. These are people who share the same value in your product that you had in creating your product, and continue to have as you promote and provide it. This shared value may present opportunities for mutually supportive collaborations and partnerships. And so, you might find yourself connecting with influencers or bloggers or people to review your product. And this might support the development of a brand culture that will bring its own benefits and opportunities for scaling. And as this puts you in touch with likeminded and like-spirited individuals, they might include people who are willing to work with you in a fractional capacity or support you in other ways.

As your plan emerges, you realize how important planning is for your leadership, management of your resources, and for communicating both your purpose and brand to others, especially if you are presenting within a capital venture pitch format. And so, you become clearer about your future, regarding sales, customers, revenue, staff and other supporters, and of course, your products, services, content, etc. In the process, you might also decide that when you reach a particular key point in your journey, and achieve its goal, that you'll introduce another product into your brand - which will then introduce yet another element into your future planning.

With your business plan developed, this leaves planning your personal life and free time. Here you find that you can actually set realistic goals for things like your personal interests, activities, pastimes, and leisure because your business planning is teaching you how to set and achieve goals within a reliable structure and system.

Once you have some clarity on your three-year goals, and one-year goals, it is then easier to fill in Key Points that are typically used in the planning process, which include your current situation, three-to-six months, nine months, the one year you've already defined, eighteen months, two years, and the three years that you've defined. And of course, all the key ideas, key qualities, traits, skills and key insights of this book can be tapped to develop your plan and achieve its goals.

Now, regarding the *Time Travel* game activity, you can use your plan to develop your timeline talks, or you can use your timeline talks to develop your plans!

Time Portal

NAME

The name, *Time Portal* refers to the idea of traveling to a timeline in your journey and giving a presentation on it from a present tense perspective (as though you are actually existing in that timeline). Your talk will be from the perspective of yourself as the entrepreneur, a customer, or a media representative.

FRAME

The frame of *Time Portal* is that of a self-selection or *online random roulette wheel* spin, in which seven Key Points of your journey correlate to numbers on the wheel. The play involves first selecting your Key Point (timeline) or discovering it on your wheel spin, then finding the correlating Key Point on the Timelines List to give your presentation. Scoring is 1 - 10 for quality of information, and 1 - 10 for the quality of your presentation, making 20 the highest possible score. (.5 decimals can be used.) The idea is that whether you are performing as yourself, or as a customer, or media representative, you should be presenting as though you are actually in the selected timeline. So, in your talk, when speaking from your future self about what you *will be* doing, etc., reference the present tense. For example, use "I am", rather than "I will".

AIM

The aim of *Time Travel* is to support the design of a comprehensive business/personal plan. And of course, the game can be played solo, with friends, family, associates, partners, or anyone interested in an entrepreneurial game that supports you or all who are playing.

And as you are developing your timeline presentation, and assuming the roles of an *entrepreneur, customer,* and/or *media representative*, you might want to consider certain descriptive words.

Here are some ideas:

POSITIVE ENTREPRENEURIAL TRAITS DISPLAYED IN THE PRESENTATION

Accommodating, Accurate, Adaptable, Admirable, Altruistic, Ambitious, Appreciative, Assertive, Attentive, Authentic, Believable, Caring, Charismatic, Collaborative, Confident, Conscientious, Considerate, Consistent, Constructive, Convincing, Cooperative, Courageous, Courteous, Creative, Credible, Decisive, Dedicated, Dependable, Determined, Diligent, Disciplined, Driven, Empathetic, Encouraging, Enthusiastic, Even-tempered, Fair-minded, Fearless, Flexible, Focused, Generous, Genuine, Good-natured, Grateful, Hard-working, Healthy, Helpful, Honest, Humble, Idealistic, Imaginative, Independent, Industrious, Innovative, Kind, Knowledgeable, Logical, Loyal, Methodical, Motivated, Nurturing, Observant, Open-minded, Optimistic, Organized, Passionate, Patient, Persistent, Persuasive, Positive, Proactive, Productive, Proficient, Purposeful, Resilient, Resourceful, Respectful, Responsible, Sincere, Skillful, Sociable, Socially Aware, Steadfast, Successful, Supportive, Tactful, Tasteful, Thoughtful, Trustworthy, Understanding, World-class, Worthy.

DESCRIPTION OF PRODUCT, BRAND, ETC. BY A CUSTOMER OR THE MEDIA

Advanced, Ahead of its time, Amazing, Attractive, Awesome, Beautiful, Best ever, Breakthrough, Classic, Clever, Commendable, Consummate, Contemporary, Cool, Creative, Cutting-edge, Distinctive, Distinguished, Dynamic, Excellent, Exceptional, Exciting, Exemplary, Exquisite, Fabulous, Finest, First-rate, Flawless, Foremost, Forward thinking, Fresh, Greatest, Groundbreaking, Incomparable, Ingenious, Innovative, Inspired, Inventive, Marvelous, New, Notable, Novel, Original, Outstanding, Pioneering, Premium, Priceless, Remarkable, Resounding, Revolutionary, Socially aware, Special, State-of-the-art, Striking, Stunning Stylish, Superb, Top-notch, Ultimate, Unsurpassed, Visionary, Wonderful, World-class.

TIMELINE PRESENTATIONS (0 – 8)

0 GRN	Give a presentation on what you are currently doing in your entrepreneurial activities.
00 GRN	Give a presentation as a customer or media person talking positively about your brand, product, service, content, etc.
1 RED	Imagining three to six months into the future, present on what you are *doing* in your entrepreneurial activities.
2 BLACK	Imagining three to six months into the future, present on what you are *thinking and/or feeling* about your brand, product, service, brand, entrepreneurial purpose, etc.
3 RED	Imagining three to six months into the future, present as a customer talking positively about you, your brand, product, service, or content.
4 BLACK	Imagining three to six months into the future, present as a customer talking positively about *the overall impact* that you, your brand, product, service, or content has had or is having on their life.
5 RED	Imagining three to six months into the future, present as a media person positively reviewing you, your brand, product, service, or content.
6 BLACK	Imagining three to six months into the future, present as a media person talking positively about *the overall impact* that you, your brand, product, service, or content has had or is having in the community, culture, society.
7 RED	Imagining nine months into the future, present on what you are *doing* in your entrepreneurial activities.
8 BLACK	Imagining nine months into the future, present on what you are *thinking and/or feeling* about your brand, product, service, brand, entrepreneurial purpose, etc.

TIMELINE PRESENTATIONS (9 – 17)

9 RED	Imagining nine months into the future, present as a customer talking positively about you, your brand, product, service, or content.
10 BLACK	Imagining nine months into the future, present as a customer talking positively about *the overall impact* that you, your brand, product, service, or content has had or is having on their life.
11 BLACK	Imagining nine months into the future, present as a media person positively reviewing you, your brand, product, service, or content.
12 RED	Imagining nine months into the future, present as a media person talking positively about *the overall impact* that you, your brand, product, service, or content has had or is having in the community, culture, society.
13 BLACK	Imagining one year into the future, present on what you are *doing* in your entrepreneurial activities.
14 RED	Imagining one year into the future, present on what you are *thinking and/or feeling* about your brand, product, service, brand, entrepreneurial purpose, etc.
15 BLACK	Imagining one year into the future, present as a customer talking positively about you, your brand, product, service, or content.
16 RED	Imagining one year into the future, present as a customer talking positively about *the overall impact* that you, your brand, product, service, or content has had or is having on their life.
17 BLACK	Imagining one year into the future, present as a media person positively reviewing you, your brand, product, service, or content.

TIMELINE PRESENTATIONS (18 – 27)

18 RED	Imagining one year into the future, present as a media person talking positively about *the overall impact* that you, your brand, product, service, or content has had or is having in the community, culture, society.
19 RED	Imagining 18 months into the future, present on what you are *doing* in your entrepreneurial activities.
20 BLACK	Imagining 18 months into the future, present on what you are *thinking and/or feeling* about your brand, product, service, brand, entrepreneurial purpose, etc.
21 RED	Imagining 18 months into the future, present as a customer talking positively about you, your brand, product, service, or content.
22 BLACK	Imagining 18 months into the future, present as a customer talking positively about *the overall impact* that you, your brand, product, service, or content has had or is having on their life.
23 RED	Imagining 18 months into the future, present as a media person positively reviewing you, your brand, product, service, or content.
24 BLACK	Imagining 18 months into the future, present as a media person talking positively about *the overall impact* that you, your brand, product, service, or content has had or is having on the community, culture, society.
25 RED	Imagining two years into the future, present on what you are *doing* in your entrepreneurial activities.
26 BLACK	Imagining two years into the future, present on what you are *thinking and/or feeling* about your brand, product, service, brand, entrepreneurial purpose, etc.
27 RED	Imagining two years into the future, present as a customer talking positively about you, your brand, product, service, or content.

TIMELINE PRESENTATIONS (28 – 36)

28 BLACK	Imagining two years into the future, present as a customer talking positively about *the overall impact* that you, your brand, product, service, or content has had or is having on their life.
29 BLACK	Imagining two years into the future, present as a media person positively reviewing you, your brand, product, service, or content.
30 RED	Imagining two years into the future, present as a media person talking positively about *the overall impact* that you, your brand, product, service, or content has had or is having in the community, culture, society.
31 BLACK	Imagining three years into the future, present on what you are *doing* in your entrepreneurial activities.
32 RED	Imagining three years into the future, present on what you are *thinking and/or feeling* about your brand, product, service, brand, entrepreneurial purpose, etc.
33 BLACK	Imagining three years into the future, present as a customer talking positively about you, your brand, product, service, or content.
34 RED	Imagining three years into the future, present as a customer talking positively about *the overall impact* that you, your brand, product, service, or content has had or is having on their life.
35 BLACK	Imagining three years into the future, present as a media person positively reviewing you, your brand, product, service, or content.
36 RED	Imagining three years into the future, present as a media person talking positively about *the overall impact* that you, your brand, product, service, or content has had or is having in the community, culture, society.

Part Seven
Key Topics

Here in Part Seven, we'll go on an expedition to find hidden treasure in the form of highly valuable ideas that can support our inner journey as compassionate, purpose-centered, and successful entrepreneurs, along with the game with the fitting name of *Search for Hidden Treasure (aka Roll & Scroll)*.

The topical ideas we'll be searching for fit into the following 12 areas:

1. Customers
2. Marketing
3. Self-Development
4. Brand
5. Professional Skills
6. Personal Leadership
7. Success
8. Social Media
9. Writing and Speaking
10. A Positive Personality
11. Higher Values
12. Mind States and Meditation

The developmental process begins with looking over the list of topics and intuitively selecting one that would be most valuable to explore at this moment in your life. Or you can roll three physical dice, or use an online dice roll randomizer to discover a topic. Let's begin with looking over the four-page list that begins on the next page.

KEY TOPIC LIST

1. CUSTOMERS

1. Serving your customers.
2. Your customers' pain points.
3. Customers' future needs.
4. Customer appreciation.
5. Your customer base.
6. Customer celebration.
7. Customer co-creation.
8. Applauding your customers.
9. Customer relationships.
10. Congregate your customer base.
11. Customers' success stories.
12. Customer education.
13. Happy customers.
14. Customer value.
15. Complimenting your customers.
16. Customer obsession.
17. Customer incubation.
18. Initiating the customer relationship.
19. Customer connection.
20. Customer surveys.
21. Customer stories.
22. Your customers' needs
23. Customer relationship management.
24. Customer confidence.
25. Customer-oriented marketing.
26. Satisfying your customers' needs.
27. Your customer promise.
28. New customers.

2. MARKETING

- Alternative marketing.
- Affiliate marketing.
- Collaborative marketing.
- Brand marketing coordination.
- Marketing correlation strategy.
- Integrated marketing.
- Marketing campaign contest.
- Using lists in marketing.
- Market domination.
- Market penetration.

3. SELF-DEVELOPMENT

- Mental focus.
- Self-presentation.
- Self-evaluation.
- Extraordinary focus.
- Self-motivation.
- Your natural talents.
- Self-liberation.
- Peak experience and performance.
- Self-reinvention.
- Personal energy renewal.
- The power of self-regulation.
- Self-exploration.
- Channeling your impulses.
- Your personal potential.
- The power of tolerance.

4. BRAND

- Positive Brand Image.
- Your Brand Culture.
- Brand administration.
- Brand explanation.
- Brand announcements.
- Articulating brand purpose.
- Bringing people into your brand culture.
- Brand association.
- Brand consistency.
- Brand marketing automation.
- Your brand's equity.
- A brand organizing technique.
- Brand communication strategy.
- Brand discussion.
- Brand strategy consolidation.
- An attractive brand concept.
- Defining your brand.
- Brand cultivation.
- Brand demonstration.
- Brand information dissemination.
- Elevating your brand.
- Brand clarity.
- Brand differentiation.
- Brand encapsulation.
- Scaling your brand.
- Brand impact.
- Brand formulation.
- Understanding your brand.
- Brand excellence.
- Brand brilliance.
- Personalize your purpose and brand.
- Humanizing your brands.
- Brand innovation.
- Brand insulation.
- Brand intimacy.
- Your brand core.
- Operating your brand.
- Brand orchestration.
- Brand orientation.
- Brand uniqueness.
- Participation branding.
- Brand permeation.
- Perpetuating your brand.
- A wider brand market reach.
- Brand publishing.
- Establishing your brand identity.
- Brand revival.
- Brand rejuvenation.
- Brand renewal.
- Being a top brand.
- Understanding your brand.
- Your brand trust.
- Your brand statement.
- Brand simplification.
- Brand variety.
- Competitor Brand differentiation.
- Brand invigoration.

5. PROFESSIONAL SKILLS

- Problem-solving.
- Team building,
- The power of decisiveness.
- Business finance.
- Idea analysis and development.
- Trend extrapolation.
- Brainstorming.
- Industry analysis.
- Strategic planning.
- Partnership.
- Panel discussion moderation.
- Partner negotiation.
- Achieving your goals.
- Business scenarios.
- Situational leadership.
- Trend watching.
- An educated guess.
- Influencer and affiliate compensation.
- Evidence-based decision making.
- Entrepreneurial delegation.
- Resource allocation.
- Staying industry current.
- Lead generation.
- Business growth.
- business strategy.
- Idea mining.
- Value & growth hypothesis.
- Successful meeting facilitation.
- Teamwork and synergy.
- The power of cooperation.
- The power of reciprocation.

6. PERSONAL LEADERSHIP

- Rapid Progress.
- Achieving your goals.
- Accumulative Advantage.
- Successful Adaptation.
- Personal business promotion.
- Creating positive circumstances.
- A good reputation.
- Making the right choices.
- Committing to your goals.
- The power of punctuality.
- The power of taking action.
- Your next level of success.
- Target audience appeal.
- The power of alone time.
- Becoming known in your field.
- The value of a strong competitor.
- Effective notetaking.
- The power of accountability
- Your official role
- A positive future.
- Self-assertiveness.

7. SUCCESS

- Expanded capacity for success.
- A success mindset.
- Success traits.
- Good success habits.
- Success modeling.
- Success duplication.
- Success emulation.
- Leveraging your success.

8. SOCIAL MEDIA

- Content publishing platforms.
- Social media interaction.
- Maximum website traffic.
- Navigating social media.
- Content syndication.
- Celebrity endorsements.

9. WRITING & SPEAKING

- Content writing technique.
- Writing commentary.
- Your company overview.
- Captivating storytelling.
- Newsworthy content.
- Motivational speaking.
- Direct and effective communication.
- The perfect speech.
- Captivating illustrations.
- Business dissertation.
- The power of repetition.

10. A POSITIVE PERSONALITY

- Your authentic self.
- Personal charisma.
- Personal magnetism.
- A positive and confident personality.
- Emanating positive energy.

11. HIGHER VALUES

- A higher mission. (A charity or cause)
- Your deeper mission. (Your brand purpose)
- A noble cause.
- Higher Self

12. MIND STATES AND MEDITATION

- The meditative mind state. (Alpha)
- Your active thinking mind state. (Beta)
- A good night's sleep. (Delta)
- The immersive mind state. (Gamma)
- A relaxed creative mind state. (Theta)
- The meditative lifestyle.
- The practice of contemplation.

Choosing your Topic

So, let use the example of 'Affiliate Marketing'. And let's say that you arrived at it either by looking over the list and choosing it, or by rolling three dice that resulted in a 1-2-4 roll. If you looked over the list and chose it, you simply do an internet search for affiliate marketing and continue as explained below. If you rolled dice, you look up the roll and find the 'Meditate and affiliate' heading / search tips.

Meditate and affiliate.
Search Tip(s): Affiliate marketing. How to find marketing affiliates. How to pay marketing affiliates.

Let's say you look at the search tips, choose, 'How to find marketing affiliates' and do a search on it. You scroll down the search results for a website that you think might produce useful results. You click the site. It comes up and you scroll its content. Keywords and phrases stand out for you, and you write them. For example:

Blogs, Product review sites, Directories, Influencers, Online communities, Customers.

You then put them in order of interest, and arrive at:

1. Online communities.
2. Product review sites.
3. Blogs
4. Influencers.
5. Customers.
6. Directories.

Finding your Ideas

When you are scrolling, the idea is to release any outside distractions and find your meditative state in which your mind is not producing random thoughts. Then without external or internal distractions, find the site that stands out for you. Then find the sections of the site. And finally, find ideas that can support your purpose, your brand, your company, your success.

The importance of the meditative approach is denoted in the fact that each Key Statement begins with the word, *Meditate*, and ends with a word that rhymes with Meditate. For example: Meditate and delegate. Meditate and innovate. Meditate and motivate. Meditate and syndicate.

Now let's dive into a fascinating theory on the practice of meditation and how the *Search for Hidden Treasure* can support our brand.

Meditation and Reading

If a goal of Meditation is for our mind not to *produce* random thoughts, the very act of reading supports this because we are not primarily *producing* thoughts. We are rather *receiving* thoughts in the form of words. And when the words enter our vision, we instantaneously access our mental language system along with our specific brand entrepreneurial journey to make a direct connection and find the keywords and ideas that can support our entrepreneurial success.

So, we first use our natural meditation skills to create a receptive mind state. And then we let our scrolling and reading lead us to the precise ideas, knowledge, and guidance to support our success.

We may not realize the extraordinary power that reading can bring into the life of an entrepreneur. So, let's look at why this might be, and how it might happen in the course of a person's life. When we are young, much of our reading occurs in connection with our school life. We are usually directed to read and learn knowledge on subjects that are part of a broad-based program designed to give us an understanding of ourselves and our world. We may not think of reading as having any great value. We are just following directions.

Along the way, we might find that we are interested in a particular topic. So, we find and read content about it on our own. And we begin to appreciate reading a bit more.

As we advance through our education, we reach a point where we are considering a particular career or profession. And then we read both general and specific information regarding our area or field. And when we take a position in our field, we then read for more specific information, and to learn applications that are required in our work.

As an entrepreneur (especially for those of us who are self-taught entrepreneurs), our reading can be precisely tailored to the needs of the moment. For example, say we are ready to form relationships with affiliates, influencers, bloggers, reviewers, etc.

We do an internet search, which provides results that lead us to more definitive searches ... which lead us to the precise information, knowledge, or guidance that we require to take action and achieve our intended or desired results. We apply what we learn, and suddenly, there are affiliates, influencers, bloggers, and reviewers who are supporting our brand.

New Topics, New Knowledge, Higher Success

As you do internet searches, you will continually be discovering new topics and new knowledge. With your Keynotes derived from your Key Quest reading and activities, (along with content from other sources), you will have your own self-developed book or file to grow your brand, and achieve and chart your success.
And finally, the spirit of game-playing keeps the journey interesting, engaging, fun, and empowering.

With the Key Quest Success Map as your real-world game board, and the Key Quest games to keep the spirit of play alive and growing, this book is not only a resource that can directly support your entrepreneurial success, but also create cooperative game playing opportunities.

As socially aware entrepreneurs, this can be so very valuable for us, as it brings into our lives a recognized and popular fun social activity, while *also* providing the opportunity for personal, social, professional, and inner development for not only *ourselves* as entrepreneurs, but for anyone involved in a purpose that can be empowered by the entrepreneurial spirit.

Search for Hidden Treasure
(aka Roll & Scroll)

NAME

The name, *Search for Hidden Treasure* derives from the idea of an expedition to find hidden treasure in the form of highly valuable ideas that can support our Inner Journey as a compassionate, purpose-centered and successful entrepreneur. And the dice rolling and online scrolling feature brings us the subtitle, *Roll & Scroll.*

FRAME

The frame of **Search for Hidden Treasure** is that of a dice game in which 216 possible dice rolls of three dice represent entrepreneurial topics. The game play involves: rolling three dice, looking up the roll and finding the topic heading and search tips. Next you look over the search tips, choose one, and do an internet search. Then you scroll down the search results and click a site that you think might produce useful results. It comes up and you scroll its content. Keywords and ideas stand out for you and present them and/or write them in your Keynotes.

AIM

The aim of *The Hero's Journey* is to support you in learning about topics that are important to your success as an entrepreneur. Of course, the game can be played solo, with friends, family, associates, partners, or anyone interested in an entrepreneurial game that supports you or all who are playing. This game also lends itself easily to a game show setting, where contestants are tested on the speed and quality of their searches.

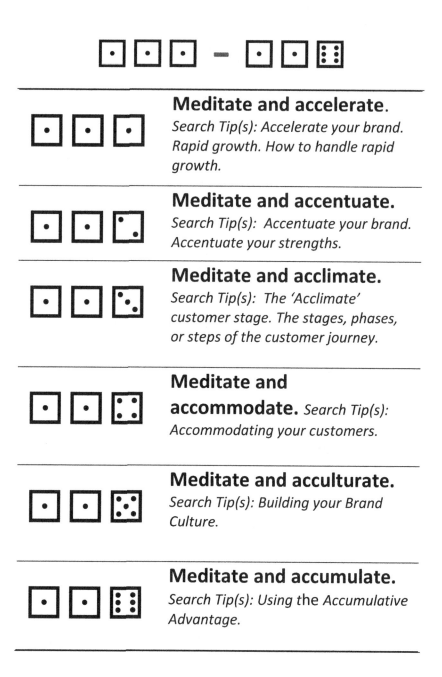

Meditate and accelerate.
Search Tip(s): Accelerate your brand. Rapid growth. How to handle rapid growth.

Meditate and accentuate.
Search Tip(s): Accentuate your brand. Accentuate your strengths.

Meditate and acclimate.
Search Tip(s): The 'Acclimate' customer stage. The stages, phases, or steps of the customer journey.

Meditate and accommodate. *Search Tip(s): Accommodating your customers.*

Meditate and acculturate.
Search Tip(s): Building your Brand Culture.

Meditate and accumulate.
Search Tip(s): Using the Accumulative Advantage.

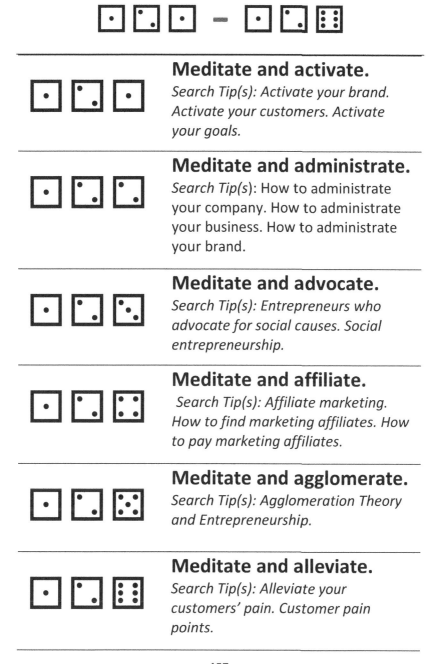

Meditate and activate.
Search Tip(s): Activate your brand. Activate your customers. Activate your goals.

Meditate and administrate.
Search Tip(s): How to administrate your company. How to administrate your business. How to administrate your brand.

Meditate and advocate.
Search Tip(s): Entrepreneurs who advocate for social causes. Social entrepreneurship.

Meditate and affiliate.
Search Tip(s): Affiliate marketing. How to find marketing affiliates. How to pay marketing affiliates.

Meditate and agglomerate.
Search Tip(s): Agglomeration Theory and Entrepreneurship.

Meditate and alleviate.
Search Tip(s): Alleviate your customers' pain. Customer pain points.

⚀⚂⚀ - ⚀⚂⚅

Meditate and alliterate.
Search Tip(s): Alliteration in marketing.

Meditate and allocate.
Search Tip(s): Allocate your marketing. Allocate your resources. Allocate your brand.

Meditate on your alpha state.
Search Tip(s): Access your alpha mind state. Benefits of the alpha mind state.

Meditate and alternate.
Search Tip(s): Alternative marketing. Alternate your marketing. Alternate your strategies.

Meditate and amalgamate.
Search Tip(s): Amalgamate your brand.

Meditate and annotate.
Search Tip(s): The benefits of annotation.

Meditate and annunciate.

Search Tip(s): Make brand announcements. Make company announcements.

Meditate and anticipate.

Search Tip(s): Anticipate your customers' needs.

Meditate and appreciate.

Search Tip(s): Appreciate your customers. Appreciate your team. Appreciate yourself.

Meditate and approximate.

Search Tip(s): Approximation for entrepreneurs.

Meditate and articulate.

Search Tip(s): Articulate your brand. Articulate your plans. Articulate your ideas.

Meditate and associate.

Search Tip(s): How to use association marketing. Build positive brand association.

Meditate on what you ate.
Search Tip(s): Meditate on what you ate. Rethink what you eat. Eat for entrepreneurial success.

Meditate and authenticate.
Search Tip(s): How to authenticate your brand. How to be authentic.

Meditate and automate.
Search Tip(s): How entrepreneurs automate. Marketing automation.

Meditate on your beta state.
Search Tip(s): Access your beta mind state. Benefits of the beta mind state.

Meditate and boilerplate.
Search Tip(s): Boilerplate your brand.

Meditate and calculate.
Search Tip(s): Entrepreneurs calculate risks.

Meditate and calibrate.
Search Tip(s): Calibrate your brand.

Meditate and capacitate.
Search Tip(s): Capacitating entrepreneurs.

Meditate and captivate.
Search Tip(s): Captivate your customers.

Meditate and celebrate.
Search Tip(s): Celebrate your customers. Celebrate your brand milestones.

Meditate and circulate.
Search Tip(s): Circulate your online content.

Meditate and have a clean slate.
Search Tip(s): Give your business a clean slate. Having a good reputation. Rebuilding a reputation.

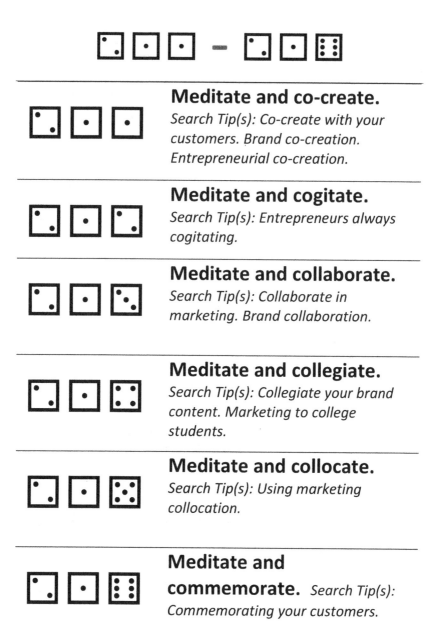

Meditate and co-create.
Search Tip(s): Co-create with your customers. Brand co-creation. Entrepreneurial co-creation.

Meditate and cogitate.
Search Tip(s): Entrepreneurs always cogitating.

Meditate and collaborate.
Search Tip(s): Collaborate in marketing. Brand collaboration.

Meditate and collegiate.
Search Tip(s): Collegiate your brand content. Marketing to college students.

Meditate and collocate.
Search Tip(s): Using marketing collocation.

Meditate and commemorate.
Search Tip(s): Commemorating your customers.

122 - 236

Meditate and commentate.
Search Tip(s): Writing successful brand commentary.

Meditate and communicate. *Search Tip(s): Communicate your brand. Brand communication strategy. Entrepreneurial communication skills.*

Meditate and compensate.
Search Tip(s): How to compensate marketing affiliates. How to compensate influencers.

Meditate and concentrate.
Search Tip(s): Concentrate your brand. Concentrate for success.

Meditate and congratulate.
Search Tip(s): Congratulate your customers.

Meditate and congregate.
Search Tip(s): Congregate your customer base. Where do your customers congregate? Congregating customer data.

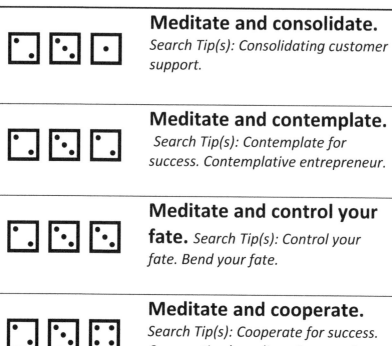

Meditate and consolidate.
Search Tip(s): Consolidating customer support.

Meditate and contemplate.
Search Tip(s): Contemplate for success. Contemplative entrepreneur.

Meditate and control your fate.
Search Tip(s): Control your fate. Bend your fate.

Meditate and cooperate.
Search Tip(s): Cooperate for success. Cooperative branding. Cooperative marketing.

Meditate and coordinate.
Search Tip(s): Coordinate your marketing. Coordinate your team.

Meditate and correlate.
Search Tip(s): Correlate your marketing. Marketing correlation strategy.

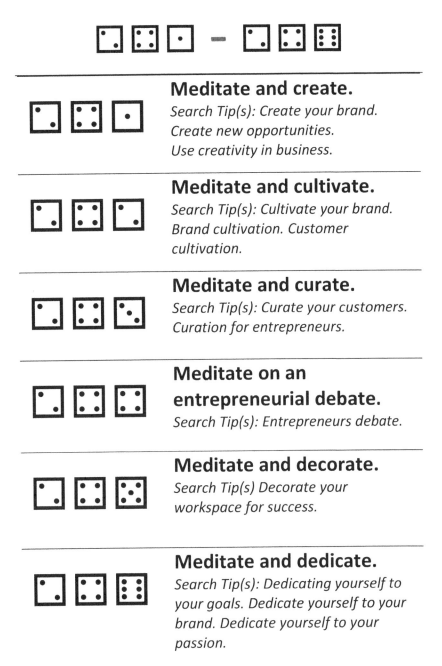

Meditate and create.
Search Tip(s): Create your brand. Create new opportunities. Use creativity in business.

Meditate and cultivate.
Search Tip(s): Cultivate your brand. Brand cultivation. Customer cultivation.

Meditate and curate.
Search Tip(s): Curate your customers. Curation for entrepreneurs.

Meditate on an entrepreneurial debate.
Search Tip(s): Entrepreneurs debate.

Meditate and decorate.
Search Tip(s) Decorate your workspace for success.

Meditate and dedicate.
Search Tip(s): Dedicating yourself to your goals. Dedicate yourself to your brand. Dedicate yourself to your passion.

163 - 156

Meditate and know your defining trait. *Search Tip(s): Know your defining trait.*

Meditate and delegate. *Search Tip(s): Delegate as an entrepreneur.*

Meditate and deliberate. *Search Tip(s): How to deliberate. Deliberate your brand. Deliberate as an entrepreneur.*

Meditate and delineate. *Search Tip(s): Delineate entrepreneurs.*

Meditate on your delta state. *Search Tip(s): Access your delta mind state. Benefits of the delta mind state.*

Meditate and demarcate. *Search Tip(s): Brand demarcation.*

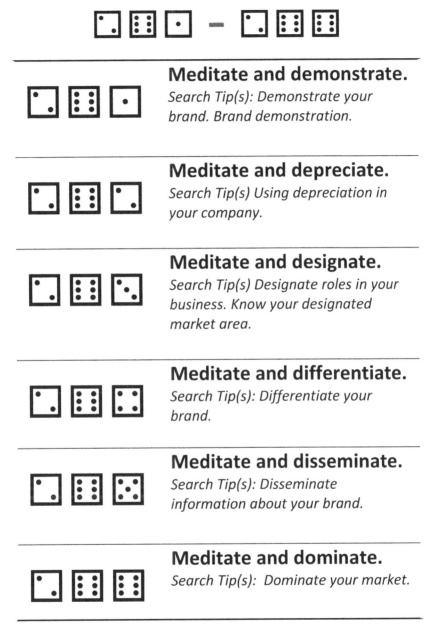

Meditate and demonstrate.
Search Tip(s): Demonstrate your brand. Brand demonstration.

Meditate and depreciate.
Search Tip(s) Using depreciation in your company.

Meditate and designate.
Search Tip(s) Designate roles in your business. Know your designated market area.

Meditate and differentiate.
Search Tip(s): Differentiate your brand.

Meditate and disseminate.
Search Tip(s): Disseminate information about your brand.

Meditate and dominate.
Search Tip(s): Dominate your market.

3 1 1 - 3 1 6

Meditate and don't be late.
Search Tip(s): Don't be late for your success.

Meditate and don't berate.
Search Tip(s): Don't berate others.

Meditate and don't exaggerate.
Search Tip(s): Don't exaggerate your brand.

Meditate and don't frustrate.
Search Tip(s): Don't frustrate yourself. How to overcome / reduce frustration.

Meditate and don't hesitate.
Search Tip(s): How to overcome hesitation.

Meditate and don't inflate.
Search Tip(s): Don't inflate your ego. Don't let your ego control you.

331 - 316

Meditate and don't isolate.
Search Tip(s): Don't isolate your brand. Don't isolate your marketing. Don't isolate your success.

Meditate and don't overestimate.
Search Tip(s): How to not overestimate yourself. How to not overestimate your time.

Meditate and don't procrastinate.
Search Tip(s): How to overcome procrastination.

Meditate and don't underestimate.
Search Tip(s): How to not underestimate yourself. How to not underestimate your time.

Meditate and donate.
Search Tip(s): Donate with your brand. Entrepreneurs donate.

Meditate and duplicate.
Search Tip(s): How to duplicate success.

Meditate and educate.
Search Tip(s): Educate your customers.

Meditate and effectuate.
Search Tip(s): Effectuate entrepreneur success.

Meditate on engagement rate.
Search Tip(s): Engagement rate. Social media engagement.

Meditate and elaborate.
Search Tip(s): Elaborate on your brand message. Elaborate on yourself.

Meditate and elate.
Search Tip(s): Keep your customers elated. Keep yourself elated.

Meditate and elevate.
Search Tip(s): Elevate your brand. Elevate your company. Elevate your purpose.

Meditate and elucidate.
Search Tip(s): Elucidate your brand. Brand clarity.

Meditate and emanate.
Search Tip(s): Emanate positivity.

Meditate and emulate.
Search Tip(s): Emulate success.

Meditate and encapsulate.
Search Tip(s): Encapsulate your brand.

Meditate and escalate.
Search Tip(s): Escalate your brand. Scaling your brand.

Meditate and enumerate.
Search Tip(s): Enumerate your brand. Enumerate your company. Enumerate your customers.

Meditate and enunciate.
Search Tip(s): How to enunciate. How to improve enunciation.

Meditate on how your customers equate.
Search Tip(s): How your customers equate.

Meditate and estimate.
Search Tip(s): Estimating project costs.

Meditate and evaluate.
Search Tip(s): Evaluate yourself. Evaluate your goals.

Meditate and exhilarate.
Search Tip(s): Entrepreneurs are exhilarated.

Meditate and explicate.
Search Tip(s): Explicate your brand. Explicate your customers. Explicate your ideas.

Meditate and extrapolate.
Search Tip(s): Extrapolate marketing trends.

Meditate and fabricate.
Search Tip(s): Fabricate a successful brand. Build a successful brand.

Meditate and facilitate.
Search Tip(s): Facilitate a successful meeting. Facilitate the buying process.

Meditate and fascinate.
Search Tip(s): Fascinate your customers.

Meditate and felicitate.
Search Tip(s): Felicitate your customers.

Meditate and fixate.
Search Tip(s): Fixate on your purpose. Fixate on your customers.

⁙ ▪ ▪ — ⁙ ▪ ⁞

Meditate and open the floodgate. *Search Tip(s): Open the floodgate for online traffic. Maximum website traffic. Optimize website for maximum traffic.*

Meditate and formulate. *Search Tip(s): Formulate your strategy.*

Meditate on the fourth estate. *Search Tip(s): Writing newsworthy content for your brand. The fourth estate.*

Meditate and fractionate. *Search Tip(s): Fractionate your brand. Factional marketing. Fractional hiring. Fractional help for your brand.*

Meditate on your gamma state. *Search Tip(s): Access your gamma mind state. Benefits of the gamma mind state.*

Meditate and generate. *Search Tip(s): Generate leads. Generate customers.*

Meditate and gestate.
Search Tip(s): Gestate your business. Venture gestation process.

Meditate and granulate.
Search Tip(s): Creating granular content.

Meditate and gravitate.
Search Tip(s): Build brand gravity.

Meditate and be great.
Search Tip(s): Be great at what you do. Brand excellence.

Meditate and guesstimate.
Search Tip(s): Guesstimating ROI. Educated guessing in business

Meditate and habituate.
Search Tip(s): Form successful entrepreneur habits.

Meditate and hibernate.
Search Tip(s): Hibernate to relax.

Meditate and hyper-concentrate. *Search Tip(s): Hyper-concentrate for success. How to hyper-focus.*

Meditate and ideate.
Search Tip(s): Ideation for business. Ideation for success. Idea Mining. Brainstorming.

Meditate and illuminate.
Search Tip(s): Illuminate your brand.

Meditate and illustrate.
Search Tip(s): Illustrate your brand.

Meditate and imitate.
Search Tip(s): The benefits of imitating for success.

Meditate and incorporate.
Search Tip(s): Incorporating your brand.

Meditate and incubate.
Search Tip(s): Incubate your business. Incubate your customers.

Meditate and inculcate.
Search Tip(s): Inculcate your marketing.

Meditate and indicate.
Search Tip(s): Indicate your success. Key performance indicators.

Meditate and individuate.
Search Tip(s): Individuate your branding.

Meditate and infatuate.
Search Tip(s): Infatuate your customers.

Meditate and initiate.
Search Tip(s): Initiate for success. Entrepreneurs initiate.

Meditate and know what's innate.
Search Tip(s): Innate traits of successful entrepreneurs.

Meditate to access your inner state.
Search Tip(s): Access your inner state.

Meditate and innovate.
Innovate your brand.

Meditate and insulate.
Search Tip(s): Insulate your brand.

Meditate and integrate.
Search Tip(s): Develop an integrated marketing approach. Create an integrated marketing campaign.

Meditate and interrelate.
Search Tip(s): Entrepreneurs interrelate. Entrepreneur groups and communities. Benefits of entrepreneur communities.

Meditate and interrogate.
Search Tip(s): Interrogate your customers. Customer surveys. Isolate objections.

Meditate and intimate.
Search Tip(s): Create brand intimacy.

Meditate and investigate.
Search Tip(s): Investigate your industry. Industry analysis.

Meditate and invigorate.
Search Tip(s): Invigorate your brand. Invigorate your business. Brand invigoration.

Meditate and invocate.
Search Tip(s): Higher self invocation.

Meditate and iterate.
Search Tip(s): Iteration of marketing. Iteration of branding. Iterative marketing. Iterative branding.

Meditate and itinerate.
Search Tip(s): Create your success itinerary. Entrepreneurial itinerary.

Meditate and liberate.
Search Tip(s): Liberate yourself for success.

Meditate and mandate.
Search Tip(s): Mandate customer success.

Meditate and have a business mate. *Search Tip(s): Having a business mate. Forming a brand partnership.*

Meditate and have a sparring mate. *Search Tip(s): Have a sparring mate in business. A sparring partner in business.*

Meditate and mitigate.
Search Tip(s): Mitigate brand risks.

Meditate and moderate.
Search Tip(s): Moderate your brand content. Panel discussion moderation.

Meditate and motivate.
Search Tip(s): Motivate your customers. Customer motivation. Brand motivation.

Meditate and narrate.
Search Tip(s): Narrate your brand. Crafting a brand narrative.

Meditate on your natural state.
Search Tip(s): Meditate on your natural state.

Meditate and navigate.
Search Tip(s): Navigating social media for your brand.

Meditate and necessitate.
Search Tip(s): How to necessitate your product.

Meditate and negotiate.
Search Tip(s): Negotiate with brand partners.

Meditate and nobilitate.
Search Tip(s): Having a noble purpose with your brand.

Meditate and nominate.
Search Tip(s): Nominate a winner with your brand. Contest marketing.

Meditate and notate.
Search Tip(s): Effective notetaking for entrepreneurs.

Meditate and nucleate.
Search Tip(s): Defining your brand's nucleus. Your brand's essence. Your brand's core values.

Meditate and numerate.
Search Tip(s): Knowing your business numbers.

Meditate and obligate.
Search Tip(s): Create obligations for success.

Meditate and operate.
Search Tip(s): Operate your business. Operating your brand. Business operations.

Meditate on your optimal state.
Search Tip(s): Finding your optimal state. Peak experience and performance.

Meditate and orate.
Search Tip(s): How to develop your oratory skills.

Meditate and orchestrate.
Search Tip(s): Brand orchestration.

Meditate and orientate.
Search Tip(s): Brand orientation.

Meditate and originate.
Search Tip(s): Originate a brand message.

Meditate and participate.
Search Tip(s): Participation branding.

Meditate and penetrate.
Search Tip(s): Penetrate your market.

Meditate and permeate.
Search Tip(s): Brand permeation. Permeate your life with passion.

Meditate and perpetuate.
Search Tip(s): Perpetuate your brand.

Meditate and populate.

Search Tip(s): Populate your customers. Customer relationship management.

Meditate and premeditate.

Search Tip(s): Premeditate your brand campaigns.

Meditate and proliferate.

Search Tip(s): Product proliferation strategy

Meditate and radiate.

Search Tip(s): Radiate positivity.

Meditate and reanimate.

Search Tip(s): Reanimate your brand.

Meditate and rebate.

Search Tip(s): How to do rebate marketing.

601 - 616

Meditate and reciprocate.
Search Tip(s): Reciprocate in business.

Meditate and recreate.
Search Tip(s): Recreate your brand. Recreate your business.

Meditate and regenerate.
Search Tip(s): Build a regenerative brand.

Meditate and regulate.
Search Tip(s): Practice self-regulation. Types of self-regulation.

Meditate and reiterate.
Search Tip(s): Use the power of repetition. Use repetition in marketing.

Meditate and rejuvenate.
Search Tip(s): Brand rejuvenation.

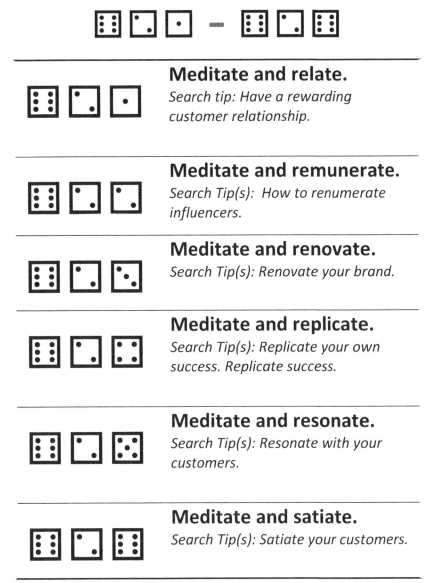

Meditate and relate.
Search tip: Have a rewarding customer relationship.

Meditate and remunerate.
Search Tip(s): How to renumerate influencers.

Meditate and renovate.
Search Tip(s): Renovate your brand.

Meditate and replicate.
Search Tip(s): Replicate your own success. Replicate success.

Meditate and resonate.
Search Tip(s): Resonate with your customers.

Meditate and satiate.
Search Tip(s): Satiate your customers.

	**Meditate and self-interrogate.** *Search Tip(s): Self-Interrogation. Self-Questioning. Self-Exploration.*
	Meditate and separate. *Search Tip(s): Separate your brand from the crowd. Being a top brand.*
	Meditate and set a date. *Search Tip(s): Set dates for achieving your goals.*
	Meditate and simulate. *Search Tip(s): Use business simulations.*
	**Meditate and situate.** *Search Tip(s): Situational leadership for the entrepreneur.*
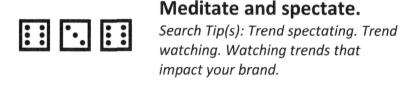	**Meditate and spectate.** *Search Tip(s): Trend spectating. Trend watching. Watching trends that impact your brand.*

Meditate and speculate.
Search Tip(s): Entrepreneurial speculation.

Meditate and find your stargate.
Search Tip(s): Star endorsements and why they work. How to find celebrities to endorse your brand.

Meditate and stimulate.
Search Tip(s): How to stimulate business growth.

Meditate and stipulate.
Search Tip(s): What to stipulate in a brand partnership agreement

Meditate and sublimate.
Search Tip(s): Sublimate aggression for success.

Meditate and substantiate.
Search Tip(s): Substantiate your brand promise. Using customer success stories.

Meditate and summate.
Search Tip(s): Create company summation.

Meditate and syndicate.
Search Tip(s): Brand content syndication.

Meditate and tabulate.
Search Tip(s): Using tables in marketing. Using tables in business.

Meditate and be a teammate. Search Tip(s): Be a business teammate.

Meditate on your theta state. Search Tip(s): Access your theta mind state. Benefits of the theta mind state.

Meditate and tolerate.
Search Tip(s): Tolerate discomfort for success. Get out of your comfort zone.

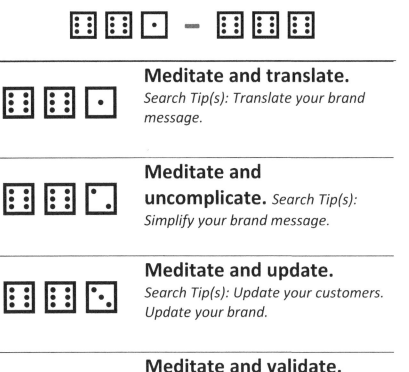

Meditate and translate.
Search Tip(s): Translate your brand message.

Meditate and uncomplicate.
Search Tip(s): Simplify your brand message.

Meditate and update.
Search Tip(s): Update your customers. Update your brand.

Meditate and validate.
Search Tip(s): Validate your customers. Validate your brand.

Meditate and valuate.
Search Tip(s): Valuate your brand. Valuate your company.

Meditate and wait.
Search Tip(s): The power of waiting. The power of patience.

Part Eight
Key Insights

Being on an inner journey means that while we are advancing in our outer everyday goals, we are also advancing in our inner development and wisdom. So, along the way, we are finding not only valuable practical knowledge regarding tangible concerns, but also inspiring insights regarding the intangibles.

Then when knowledge and insight come together,
we have the best of both worlds.

Here in Part Eight of *Key Quest - The Inner Journey of the Entrepreneur*, we will look at 21 Key Insights and their direct benefits; and also consider their indirect benefit of inspiring us to discover our own insights as we travel the inner journey.

So here we will find 21 gems filled with insights.
Then in the game version, we will use the word GEM as an acronym for, "Great entrepreneurship means ..."

For example, let's look at the first Key Insight and the first GEM – 'Great entrepreneurship means accessing intuitive ideas and insights to support our purpose.'

- Insightful thinking regarding this topic takes us through its metaphor and brings us into a deeper meaning and understanding of the process of 'idea mining'.

- The metaphor is that we are mining for something of value when we travel into the inner caverns of our imagination and intuition. We are on an inner excavation. And when we take a deeper dive into the traditional mining and excavation concept, we find three types: surface mining, placer mining, and underground mining. In our first Key Insight, we explore these as they symbolize types of *idea* mining; and they provide us with a more profound meaning and deeper understanding of the idea mining process.

As you travel through these pages, you will find practical points addressing entrepreneurial topics, such as those found in the first seven Key Insights.

And then there are the deeper dives, such as those found in the Key Insights 8 through 14.

And then we go even deeper in the Key Insights 15 through 21, with titles like, *'We are all Connected'*, *'Imagination and Manifestation'*, "Our Innermost Being," and finally, "Peace, Love, and Truth."

And so, insightful thinking means that we dive into a topic. Of course, your practice of meditation gives you the advantage of being able to access your inner self and this kind of thinking more naturally and easily.

As a developmental process, you can just simply read through the 21 Key Insights in sequence. On the next three pages, you will find the list to reference. And following the list, you will find an overview of the game version of the 21 Key Insights in the game, *21 GEMs*.

The Key Insights (1 - 7)

1. **Idea Mining**
   Great entrepreneurship means accessing intuitive ideas and insights to support our purpose.

2. **The Accumulative Advantage**
   Great entrepreneurship means leveraging success to achieve greater success.

3. **Affiliate Marketing**
   Great entrepreneurship means affiliating with other entrepreneurs to help others.

4. **Entrepreneurial Delegation**
   Great entrepreneurship means knowing how to effectively and tactfully delegate.

5. **Collaborative Marketing**
   Great entrepreneurship means collaborating with other entrepreneurs to help others.

6. **Marketing Automation**
   Great entrepreneurship means knowing how to automate marketing.

7. **Reaching a New Level of Success**
   Great entrepreneurship means reaching new levels of success.

The Key Insights (8 - 14)

8 People and Purpose
Great entrepreneurship means understanding our inner purpose in relation to others.

9 Your World of Purpose
Great entrepreneurship means understanding our inner purpose in relation to the outer everyday world.

10 Positive Personal Qualities
Great entrepreneurship means having positive *personal* qualities that support both your inner development and your outer success.

11 Positive Social Qualities
Great entrepreneurship means having positive *social* qualities that support both your inner development and your outer success.

12 Self-Reinvention
Great entrepreneurship means that we can reinvent ourselves to become exactly who we want to be.

13 Carpe' Diem (Seizing the Day)
Great entrepreneurship means living in the present, while learning from the past, and planning the future.

14 Positive Expectancy
Great entrepreneurship means being prepared for great things to happen.

The Key Insights (15 - 21)

15 We are all Connected
Great entrepreneurship acknowledges the vast connectedness and relationship of all life.

16 Interpretation and Attitude
Great entrepreneurship means keeping our interpretations constructive and our attitude positive.

17 Drawing Meaning from our Reality
Great entrepreneurship means drawing personal meaning from everyday reality that supports our purpose.

18 Discovery and Creation
Great entrepreneurship means experiencing purpose as a process of discovery and creation.

19 Imagination and Manifestation
Great entrepreneurship means practicing the power of imagination and manifestation.

20 Our Innermost Being
Great entrepreneurship means being on an inner journey, and knowing that the path to our innermost being is in each eternal moment.

21 Peace, Love, and Truth
Great entrepreneurship means aspiring to peace, love, and truth through our purpose, mission, and vision.

21 GEMs

NAME
The name, *21 GEMs,* refers to the 21 Key Insights' introductory sentences that all begin with the words, "Great entrepreneurship means …" for which GEM is an acronym.

FRAME
The frame of *21 GEMs* is that of a self-selection or online 1-21 number wheel game, in which the Key Insights follow the numbers on the wheel. The play involves selecting your Key Insight, or discovering your number from your wheel spin and finding the correlating insight. Then you read the Key Insight and share how you can apply it to your life, or build upon it with your own intuitive ideas.

AIM
The aim of *21 GEMs* is to get in touch with your *inner* entrepreneurial nature. Going deeper in this way can get us in touch with the power of intuition, and open doors to great entrepreneurial development. When we consider history's geniuses and our most celebrated innovators, we find that they relied on their intuition and insightful thinking. So, 21 GEMs is meant to stimulate this kind of thinking, while providing 21 examples. Of course, the game can be played solo, with friends, family, associates, partners, etc., and can involve a set number of insights to be scored. A four-star model can be used, replacing stars with token gems. For example: Sapphire = 1 (Good), Ruby = 2 (Very Good), Emerald = 3 (Excellent), and Diamond = 4 (Amazing), with gems totaled at the conclusion to determine the winner(s).

- Key Insight 1 -
Idea Mining

Great entrepreneurship means accessing intuitive ideas and insights to support our purpose.

Progress. Advancement. Improvement. Relevance. These keep a brand and a company moving forward and staying successful. And the way they happen is through ideas that support the goals of the brand and the company. When we think of where ideas originate, we can think of them as being located in a mine, and the work is to excavate – to mine the ideas. Let's look at how gold is mined to make the process even more fun and interesting.

- Surface mining is used for more shallow and less valuable deposits.
- Placer mining is the sifting of gold from other sediments.
- Underground mining is used to reach deeper richer deposits.

Mining for gold is about the goal of wealth. So, the first thing to do is define the goal for which you are mining ideas. When you have defined the goal(s), you can begin. We can then surface mine by looking at what we are already doing it and extracting ideas related to it. We can placer mine by looking at what others are doing and sifting out ideas relevant to our own purpose. And then we can underground mine where the most value deposits of ideas are found.

We can mine for valuable ideas by using a mind map as our treasure map. Write the goal in a circle in the middle of a page, and extend veins from it.

Next, clear your mind. When thoughts arise, let them subside – except for thoughts related to your goal. Wait for the valuable ideas to come, and write them on the veins. This is using the power of meditation to release irrelevant thoughts so that the valuable ideas can be mined.

To prepare for the process, hold each of the following key questions lightly in your mind for a few moments. Then let go of the question, meditate, and wait for answers to come.

- What is a goal that you want to achieve?
- Why is this goal important for your brand or company?
- What are objectives that must occur for you to achieve the goal? You may want to work backwards on this, discovering the objective immediately preceding your goal, than one before that, and so on.

  With these answers, mine for ideas, strategies, action items, etc. to support the achievement of your goal and its objectives.

- Key Insight 2 -
The Accumulative Advantage

Great entrepreneurship means leveraging success to achieve greater success.

The accumulative advantage occurs when a small advantage at the beginning of something leads to an opportunity that makes a bigger difference; and then that advantage leads to another opportunity, and so on. Common phrases referring to the accumulative advantage are snow-ball effect, cascade effect, domino effect, exponential growth. So, essentially it is the continuing and spreading of results. Supporting the success of your brand are the accumulation of:

- Knowledge on how to communicate your brand.
- Skills on the operation of your brand.
- Content that explains the benefits of your brand.
- Content that *proves* the benefits of your brand.
- Presence of your brand online.
- Brand ambassadors, affiliates, and other supporters.

Begin by defining how your purpose helps people, and imagining the number of people being helped expanding until you have made a genuine difference in the world. So, the ultimate accumulation is the accumulation of the goodness of your purpose in how it helps more and more people. Consider how you can use the accumulative advantage in your brand.

- Key Insight 3 -
Affiliate Marketing

Great entrepreneurship means affiliating with other entrepreneurs for mutual gain.

Affiliate marketing is a process by which a person earns a form of income for marketing your products are services.

Four types of affiliate marketing you can consider include:

Influencers. An influencer can impact your potential customers' decision to purchase your product.

Bloggers. A Blogger might sample your product and then writes a review on it.

Email lists. You can use your own email list to promote your product or connect with affiliates who send out emails that includes a link to your website.

Recognized social media. These are the big platforms. You know them. They can provide focused targeting to your specific customer group.

And sites with which you can affiliate include:
- Coupon sites
- News & media sites
- Review sites
- Loyalty sites
- Shopping comparison sites

- Key Insight 4 -
Entrepreneurial Delegation

Great entrepreneurship means knowing how to effectively and tactfully delegate.

As an entrepreneur, you are a doer. At some point, you realize that there are certain things that others can do better, or tasks that others can perform to give you time to do other things. And so, it is time to delegate.

Begin by being clear at a granular level on exactly why you want to delegate a task, function, or role to an employee, an outside professional, or other party. This means why it is *personally* important to you, besides your professional reasons.

Once you have reached this clarity, the next step is to define how your business will grow and change, and what you can do to prepare for the growth and the changes.

Then you are ready to search for and find the person or people who can share your commitment, passion, and focus on the results required of the role.

Now it's time to find the sweet spot regarding the type and level of oversight required to assure optimal performance and productivity. To prepare for this, you can address it in your interviews and initial meetings, and learn their own style and preferences.

- Key Insight 5 -
Collaborative Marketing

Great entrepreneurship means collaborating with other entrepreneurs for mutual benefit.

Collaborative marketing is connecting your brand's resources with another brand to support your goals. A first step in collaboration is to identify a brand that has the same or similar types of customers, and that you are interested in for a collaboration. Since you may be sharing customers, you probably would not choose one in direct competition with your brand. Brainstorm by imagining your customer, and what other kinds of products they would naturally have in their lives.

Once you decide on a potential collaborator, it's time to reach out to them and share your mission, why you chose them, what you like about their product, their brand, etc. And once you set the groundwork, make your offer and ask for their decision. Forms of collaboration include:

- Posts about the partnering brand.
- Podcasts where you share information about your shared values.
- Social media collaborations where you both receive a form of income on sales that are generated by the other.
- And of course, there is the traditional retail partnership with your product on their physical or virtual shelf space.

- Key Insight 6 -
Marketing Automation

*Great entrepreneurship means knowing
how to automate marketing.*

Marketing automation is using technology to manage marketing processes and campaigns automatically, and in turn, more efficiently and profitably.

So, let's begin with **social media**. Social media automation uses tools to schedule posts in advance, and to expand your social media presence by automating your content curation, that is, searching, selecting, commenting on, and sharing with your audience content already available on a specific subject to support your followers.

A landing page is a page connected to your website designed to create interest and collect information from a visitor. Automating your landing page means coordinating it with your other marketing platforms so that a visitor moves seamlessly from a marketing platform to the page.

And **email marketing automation** involves scheduling emails so they can be sent automatically within certain intervals or timeframes.

To find tools for automation, you can search social media automation, content curation automation, landing page automation, and/or email automation tools.

- Key Insight 7 -

Reaching a New Level of Success

*Great entrepreneurship means
reaching new levels of success.*

⚷

Reaching a new level of success can be exciting. And it can be daunting. The exciting part of it can drive you forward. The daunting part can bring unwanted stress into your life. The stress might be caused by being somewhat unprepared for your new situation and the new 'you'. So, let's take a look at what will be happening as you advance to that new level.

You will be doing new things - new activities and tasks. You will be letting go of some old activities and tasks. And you will continue some things you have been doing.

There will be new people in your life. There will be some of the same people in your life. And there will be people with whom you may have little or no contact.

You may require new personal traits and qualities. And you may have to let go of old habits to accommodate your higher functioning. You will most likely feel differently about yourself in some way. And your new level of success may affect your personal life or other areas of your life.

Knowing that such changes may be occurring helps you to be ready for them when they do occur. Making notes in a journal may be very helpful through your transition.

- Key Insight 8 -
People and Purpose

*Great entrepreneurship means
understanding our purpose
in relation to others.*

⊝╌

We are entrepreneurs on an inner journey. We practice meditation to access our inner nature and intuitive insights to support our purpose. With our inner nature acknowledged, our inner practice in place, and an important purpose of our life clarified, we can look at the people in our life through an intuitive perspective.

The idea is to see why certain people are in our life, and the roles they may be playing in our inner development and the fulfillment of our purpose. And this might be that certain people are simply role models of positive qualities.

Then there are those who directly support us in our own purpose and the achieving of our goals. And of course, there are the people whom we are helping as part of our purpose.

Then there are those who might challenge us. Some might make us self-reflect to see our flaws *along with* our strengths. And some might actually show us how *not* to be and what *not* to do by the examples of their own transgressions or mistakes, etc.

In our process of understanding the meaning of people in our life, we can begin with the people closest to us and then expand outward to any and all people who are somehow connected to our purpose and goals.

And of course, besides our existing circle of people, we can discover new people, or kinds of people, to add to our life to support our inner journey and the realization of our purpose and goals.

When we begin making a list of people, we can then take our time to explore the meaning they represent in our life, and how we want to proceed regarding them.

And of course, meditation can support the process with intuitive ideas and insights.

- Key Insight 9 -
Your World of Purpose

*Great entrepreneurship means
understanding our inner purpose
in relation to the outer everyday world.*

⊶

As compassionate, purpose-centered entrepreneurs, we are learning to see ourself and other people in a meaningful and purposeful way. A next step is to see our world - the places, things, events, and activities as all having meaning and purpose. In other words, what do they reveal that might support us on our inner journey and support us in living our purpose and fulfilling our personal destiny?

Places in our life might involve people and where they gather, such as a place of business, a home office, a work site, a client's location, etc. Or they might simply be natural spaces such as particular landscapes that we visit. *Things* might include our phone and other devices, our car, our clothes, our meals. Events and activities might involve our actions and interactions.

Making a list will reveal so much about us and our world, what's important to us, and perhaps adjustments we may want to make in our life. We might also find ourself reorganizing our life, decluttering, streamlining, etc. These are all in line with the simplifying process of finding one's purpose.

The minimalist lifestyle is a trend that is growing in popularity; and might be useful in living a life of purpose in that we reduce or remove items in our life that do not serve our purpose or our overall wellbeing. For many minimalists, the philosophy is about disposing of excess possessions and living life based on experiences rather than worldly possessions. Of course, the inner path is about just that – inner or personal experiences being more important or more essential than possessing material *things*.

Places, things, events, and activities might also exist in the digital reality of the internet or a wide spectrum of technological and virtual formats including Virtual, Augmented, and Mixed Reality that simulate reality in various ways.

As people are spending more and more time online, it may be valuable to dive a bit deeper here. The digital natives who grew up online have a full sense of existing in an actual place while online. In a way, the internet *as a place* resonates with a kind of an inner reality since it is a plane that can feel transcendent to the physical plane of material life.

So, when we're online, it doesn't feel as though we are *using* a technology as much as it feels like we are *going to* different locations, connecting with people, doing things, and, in some cases living completely different lives, with online personas that people can recognize as us (as in games and online forums).

And so, when we consider the places of our life, we would include those *virtual* places where people gather and communicate with one another in real time - those virtual places that all have their own character and kinds of people who frequent them - those virtual places that transcend the concept of distance by bringing people together in the feeling of a tangible shared experience, people who might actually be hundreds or thousands of miles apart in the physical world.

With the realization that we can include our *online* experiences and transactions, we can take some quiet time to reflect on this amazing world in which we live - in its actual physical sense, its virtual sense, and whatever other perspective we may want to include.

We can begin making a list of important places in our life, their meaning and purpose, and our personal experience of them. We can select a few of the most important or most necessary places to begin the process. We can also include new places we are adding, or would like to add to our world.

And we can do the same process with the things, the events, and the activities of our world.

The places, the things, and the activities of our everyday world define our everyday existence. When we strive to know our world, understand it, and appreciate it, then we may discover its ultimate secrets, and its place in our purpose and personal destiny.

- Key Insight 10 -
Positive Personal Qualities

*Great entrepreneurship means
having positive personal qualities
that support both our inner development
and our outer success.*

⊶

With the practice of Meditation, there are four personal qualities that naturally develop and support both our inner development and our outer success. These are Patience, Awareness, Composure, and Equanimity.

So, as for *Patience*, this quality means that we are gaining mastery over the passing of time. That's a pretty deep definition. And it means that we don't get ruffled when unexpected things happen, which can actually happen fairly often. And we don't get tangled up in useless worry. We give things the time they take to happen.

Now when we apply our power of patience to the passing moments of time, those moments hold certain items that we experience. And we can either resist these items or we can accept them for either the positive experience they bring, or something to learn from a negative experience they might contain. With acceptance, we are in control. For even with the negatives of life, we observe how they affect us, learn from them, and grow from them. So, we practice *Acceptance* and we move along our path.

And then with Patience and Acceptance, we find a third quality naturally developing, and that is a sense of *Composure*. When you think about it, composure really has two meanings. One is the obvious, which is a sense of inner calm. And the other may be more practical, in that composure provides a sense of feeling ready for whatever might come next. And so, with Patience, Acceptance, and Composure, we can take life as it comes and stay pretty calm through all of it, or at least with much more of it than if we didn't have these qualities. So now we're feeling quite confident and competent, full of inner calm power. And suddenly something comes up that is a bit more challenging.

That's where the final quality of *Equanimity* comes into play. Our key definition is *letting things come and go and remaining in, or returning to, our sense of composure.* Challenges can be personal, social, work related. They can be medium, large, extra-large, or cataclysmic, such as a tsunami or pandemic or any life-or-death situation.

So, with our outer everyday life as our playing field, we can always level the playing field by remembering the keyword, PACE, and accessing our inner qualities of Patience, Acceptance, Composure, and Equanimity … and the phrase 'pace yourself'.

- Key Insight 11 -
Positive Social Qualities

*Great entrepreneurship means
having positive social qualities that support
both our inner development and our outer success.*

From the practice of Meditation, there are four personal qualities that naturally develop and support both our inner development and our outer success. These are the PACE qualities of Patience, Acceptance, Composure and Equanimity.

When we take our PACE qualities and our inner calm into our social experience, we find four qualities naturally developing that form the acronym, CARE.

C is for *Compassion*, which is a feeling that shows someone that you care, and that you want to be a true friend and support.

A is for *Acknowledgement*, which is an act or expression of recognizing someone's value and self-worth, and that shows you appreciate them for who they are.

R is for *Respect*, which is a feeling toward someone that says you accept them for their personal qualities, abilities, achievements, position, etc.

E is for *Encouragement*, which is the act or expression of offering or providing support, confidence, or hope to someone.

And so, we have Compassion, Acknowledgement, Respect, and Encouragement, whose initials combine to create our keyword, CARE. The more firmly grounded we are in these qualities, the easier it is to see the people and the world in a positive way, and create positive conditions and results for all involved. So, with our positive social qualities, we care for others.

By starting our day remembering the key words, PACE and CARE, we can stay centered in our positive personal and social qualities and recall them as needed in the midst of all the challenges and potential turbulence of the outer everyday world.

- Key Insight 12 -
Self-Reinvention

*Great entrepreneurship means
that we can reinvent ourselves
to become exactly who we want to be.*

⚷

In the natural course of our lives, we invent ourselves, usually with the help of others who affect and condition our thoughts, feelings, and behavior. Sometimes the invention of our 'self' continues on in its original form. And sometimes, we look to reinvent our 'self'.

As meditators, we can be more inclined to self-invention since we get to look at ourselves and our lives more clearly and intuitively through the meditative state. In meditation, we observe how the outer world is often all about cause and effect, from the wonderful things that happen like having a family to the worst things like conflict and war. And as we *deepen* our meditation, we realize that when we access our inner world, that we have a choice. We don't need to be controlled by outer events. We can choose what we want to keep in our life, what to remove, what we want to change, who we want to be.

Since our new self will be the 'social' self that we want to people to experience, we'll begin with the realization that as social beings, we have been influenced and conditioned by the people in our life, what they mean to us, how we relate to them, how our memory of them impacts our life.

Parents, relatives, friends, neighbors, schoolmates, teachers, coaches, coworkers, employers. Consider the influence that these people have had. Now imagine that *everyone* in our life represents a lesson to support our success. This is a goal of entrepreneurial self-*reinvention* - to repurpose our social memories to support the success of our brand and our mission of helping others.

So, with our 100% commitment to our purpose and our mission of helping others, we redefine our lives. And we begin with defining how certain people have positively contributed to our success, either by what they have taught us, or simply by being positive role models

As we identify more and more people in this way, we may come across names that represent a negative experience, either originating from the other person or from us. These memories can also be valuable. To derive this value, we can identify the negativity within the memory, and then identify an opposite quality, which we could then represent. So, say we come across an unscrupulous person who harmed us financially in some way. We might ask, "How can I myself be more honest and ethical?" Or if we have a memory of a mean-spirited person, we might ask, "How can I myself be more kind or thoughtful?"

Perhaps the greatest challenge to positively repurposing negative experiences is when we initiated or contributed to the negativity. In this case, we can once again identify the nature of the negativity, define the opposite, and look at how we can represent the positive. So, if we did something that created a negative impact, we look for a way to create an opposite impact going forward.

This means confronting ourself, rising above our ego defenses and needs, and looking at ourself objectively. When we are in the true spirit of helping others with our brand, we are rising above our own ego needs.

It is truly a hero's journey when we do battle with the negative forces of the world, especially when it is an inner battle to refine our own character. And since it is an inner battle, victory is not about defeating the other or oneself; it is about learning, changing, growing, and being a better person. And in this way, as we make ourselves better, we can be authentic in expressing and sharing our intention to make *the world* a better place.

Now let's consider that in the course of these activities, you are actually developing the skill of thinking about people and attributing a value to them. This is done in the field of sports with player statistics. We can also find it in other fields where people are reviewed using a statistical model. With your *entrepreneurial* focus, you do this with people related to your purpose, and apply *systems thinking* to the process. And in this way, you find you can manage an increasing amount of social data. So, for example, if you have an initial goal to help 10,000 people with your product, service, content, or brand, your ability to somehow mentally manage that number of people or their social data will support you in achieving your goal.

And this leads us to a very practical benefit. And that is that you are learning how to expand your social *capacity*, and use it to support the success of your brand and your purpose of helping others

- Key Insight 13 -
Carpe' Diem (Seizing the Day)

Great entrepreneurship means living in the present,
while learning from the past,
and planning the future.

⚷

Every morning, we awake into an inner, subjective reality, composed of thoughts, feelings, and sensations that make up our experience. This is where our inner purpose resides.

And every morning, we awake into an outer, objective reality – composed of seconds, minutes, hours that make up our day. This is the realm of the everyday world.

When we arrive at a singular purposeful focus in our life, our inner and outer realities blend, and we can seize the day and experience a unified sense of power. Our energy becomes indomitable. The earth becomes our home - a place that provides all the positive experiences that a home should bring. We view people clearly as they relate to our purpose and intention of helping others. Our life, even with its many varied and dynamic activities, takes on a meditative quality, as distractions subside, and deep positive values emerge.

And when we take the outer world meditative state back into our inner practice of meditation, our practice advances at an accelerated pace.

Once this blend of inner meditation practice and an outer world meditative state is established in our life, when we awaken into a day, we awaken into a new reality. We leave behind our old world of everyday motivations and the people, places, and things associated with those motivations. Now all our motivation and all the people, places, and things in our life are in harmony.

There is no conflict when our reality is unified in purpose. The world is our world. The day is our day. And so, we initiate interactions and we evaluate people in terms of how they support, and how they are supported by our purpose. We evaluate resources by how they support our purpose of helping others. We evaluate our activities accordingly, and also on how they enhance our physical, mental, emotional, and motivational energy to support our purpose.

So, not only do our direct purposeful activities support our purpose, but also things like nutrition, exercise, good sleep, of course, meditation, and anything that hones our human instrument and aligns it to our purpose.

And when our inner and outer realities are blended in this way, somehow the right people, places, and things are attracted to us and our purpose. Whatever process underlies this phenomenon, it is generally believed to be a valid active process that occurs in the lives of extraordinarily focused and committed individuals. We know such extraordinary individuals since many of them are celebrated for their commitment and their achievements in their careers, professions, crafts, etc.

So, we can experience self-empowerment every day in our purposeful life by adopting the key phrase, 'carpe-diem' – seize the day. Seizing the day is an affirmation and intention that we will 'make the very most of our day'. It usually happens before our day begins or when it is starting. Having intentions and preset goals for our day supports our ability to go into the day with a strong sense of intention and steadfastness.

Excellence occurs more readily and easily within such a day because we are functioning and performing within the momentum of our affirmation and our higher intention. Following the law of inertia, something in motion tends to stay in motion. So, when we begin our day in full higher awareness with the intention of being totally involved in our purpose of helping others, that intention will keep us moving in a positive direction throughout our day, and further deepen our awareness in the process.

By nature, we are filled with energy, and our energy naturally looks for a channel. So, if we don't provide a channel with our own higher intention, our energy can easily find its way into lower motivations and activities. The idea is to let our intention be known, let our mind be clear, let our heart shine, and let our day flow.

When we establish a morning meditation, habit, or ritual of seizing the day, we know that it will shape how we experience the hours ahead.

And then, we can look back on our day,
and know that we made the very most of it.

- Key Insight 14 -
Positive Expectancy

*Great entrepreneurship means
being prepared for great things to happen.*

With our everyday logical thinking minds, we can find life to be somewhat predictable. But when we access our inner nature and connect to our intuitive source, we open the door to a transcendent process that is beyond our everyday linear and sequential thinking minds. And so, we might find new surprising things happening in our life.

New unexpected people might appear. New insights and innovations might be revealed. New resources might be discovered. We might think of it all as serendipity, kismet, good luck, etc. Whatever our reference, when such positive events, situations, and outcomes occur more regularly, we begin to *expect* them to continue happening. We develop positive expectancy, and with each occasion, we develop more preparedness to make the most of all the good fortune that is coming our way.

And when these positive events, situations, outcomes, etc. do then happen, our best approach is to just let them happen, be grateful and humble, and continue our inner practice to continue connecting to our intuitive source.

In other words, we settle into our new reality, and get comfortable in it. We claim our new status, our new position, our new life.

- Key Insight 15 -
We are all Connected

*Great entrepreneurship means
sensing our connectedness
and the relationship of all life.*

⚬—⚬

If there is one ultimate truth to which we can all agree regardless of our beliefs or traditions, it is that we exist in connection, and through our connection with others.

Within time and space, this is our reality. Through time we are connected to our parents, their parents, *their* parents, and back to the beginning of the entire generational process. And through space, with our homes, neighborhoods, towns, cities, countries, and the entire world, we are connected with our families, neighbors, fellow citizens, and ultimately, all the people on our planet. We refer to ourselves with titles that define our relationships – mothers, fathers, daughters, sons, sisters, brothers, as well as work and professional titles, political, religious, and other group affiliation titles.

There is a title and a connection that is most relevant to us as entrepreneurs. It is the title of 'customer' or 'client'. It is the reason that our own professional title exists. As entrepreneurs, our purpose provides us with this unique connection in which we share a particular value in a give-and-take or giving-and-receiving relationship.

This relationship actually begins before the fact with the inner gifts we have *received*, as in our talents and aptitudes that lead to our developing traits and skills to support a particular purpose in life. And then, with those traits and skills, we *give* of ourselves in the spirit of helping others. And with this giving of ourselves, others receive. They receive products, services, content, and features that bring benefits.

So, one side of this social connection comes from valuing something to the degree that we either create it and/or distribute it. And the other side of the social connection is that someone values the product, service, content, or brand to the degree that they purchase it, acquire it, obtain it -receive it, along with its benefits.

Some of our latest research reveals that people form personal relationships with the products, services, and content they purchase. This is because their use of it says something about them. It can represent a personal value, a belief, a lifestyle, an association with a particular population or group. With this knowledge, we realize the important part that we play in a person's life with our product, service, content, or brand, in the way we present it, and in the customer's journey of acquiring and using it.

We are acting in the service of others - in the service of our customers. To do this well, we must know what our customers want - the problem they want to solve, the experience they want to have, the population or group with whom they want to be associated.

And so, our customers want something - they have a desire and intention. Their want is like the wind or the wave; and we are the sailor or the surfer. And the experience that we are seeking is that feeling of letting go and letting our customers' wants and needs bring us into the flow, being carried by the energy of our customers' desires and intentions.

The motivation and inspiration of an entrepreneur on their Key Quest is about shifting from self-serving action to other-serving action. However, the beauty and elegance of this theory and practice is that the benefit that our *customer* values in the receiving and use of the product is the same benefit that we value in the creation and/or distribution of the product. And so, the harmony of two people become the unity of the one value.

And when we create an inner world based on the value, a world where all the players and people involved share the value through their various roles and positions, we create a unified field. Existing, living, and performing within the field becomes a personally satisfying, empowering, and enjoyable experience. And the further we go into this experience, the more sublime and elevated it becomes, resulting in an ultimate experience and inner states of being that derive from the experience.

So, we are all connected. And within our connection with all people, there are those people with whom we share values that are expressed through our products, services, or content. They represent a door to open that leads us to the full experience of our human connectedness.

- Key Insight 16 -
Interpretation and Attitude

*Great entrepreneurship means
keeping our interpretations constructive
and our attitude positive.*

⚯

To dive into this intriguing idea, let's first consider the following inner theory regarding human life:

>It is our *interpretation of*,
>and our *attitude towards,*
>the events in our everyday world
>that are most vital.

The events of our life can give us a sense that we are moving toward our personal destiny, or away from it. So, in this regard, it is the feeling that we are being drawn toward our personal destiny, or being drawn away from it that indicates our progress on the path. Therefore, with the right interpretation of, and the right attitude toward what is occurring, our personal destiny will become clearer, and we'll develop and deepen our inner nature.

To prepare to dive deeper, let's first now note that our ultimate inner achievement comes when we realize that there is *initially* our inner nature, and it is *that* from which our purpose and personal destiny are deriving. And our only sense of volition in our outer world concerns whether we are moving in agreement with our inner purpose and personal destiny or not.

So, within this thinking, how do we interpret those times when we might stray from the path - deviate, digress, diverge, miss the point, get sidetracked, etc.? If all of it initiates from our inner nature, then the straying *is part of* the inner process. And the reason for it is to learn how to adjust, refine, rethink, reinvent, regroup, go deeper, etc.

This is a real, legitimate, and important part of the inner process, since so much can be learned and discerned in this parallel area that can elevate us even further when we resume on the path. So, the idea is not to criticize or undervalue ourself if we stray from the path or make mistakes. The idea is to realize that our *value* through all of the changes remains constant, since our purpose and personal destiny are constant. The idea is to simply remain composed, stoic and resolute regarding our purpose of helping others.

And as it is with times that we *stray from* the path, so it is with the times when we *stay on* the path.

So, when we are precisely on point, perfect and flawless in the implementation of our plans, the idea is not to praise or overvalue ourself because we are staying on the path; and to realize that our value through all of our achievement remains constant, since our purpose and our spirit of helping others are constant.

In other words, whether we are *staying on* our path or *straying from* our path, the idea is to remain composed, stoic and resolute regarding our purpose of helping others and fulfilling our personal destiny.

- Key Insight 17 -
Drawing Meaning from our Reality

*Great entrepreneurship means
drawing personal meaning from everyday reality
that supports our purpose.*

⚬━

There are various theories regarding the concept of 'destiny'. They include terms like predetermination, cause and effect, free will, choice. References include religion, philosophy, spirituality, psychology, neuroscience, and quantum physics. Whatever theory we support, there remains the fact that in reality, things happen to us. Some we consider positive, some negative. Some wonderful, and some horrible. Some extraordinarily fortunate and some completely disastrous. These things simply happen, and many seem to be beyond our control.

In all of our theories, a consistent principle is that our reality is in some way determined before we were born, either by a natural or supernatural process. And so, once we begin our life, we cannot choose another reality. Then it is within the life we are living and its reality that we find its people, places, things, events, and activities.

And here is a basic principle of our personal destiny as channeled through our human life.

> *"Whatever meaning we draw from our reality affects how we will then proceed."*

In meditation, we access our inner nature, beyond our ego mind. So, in our purposeful activities, if we draw a meaning that aligns with our inner nature and we act upon that meaning, we experience more of our inner nature, and naturally align to our spirit of helping others. If we draw a meaning that doesn't align with our *inner* nature and we act upon that meaning, we may experience more of our *ego* nature.

Our perspective, whether originating from our inner nature our ego nature, determines the way we act, interact and react. It determines the people, places, and things that we let remain in our lives, or let go from our lives. It determines new people, places, and things that we bring into our lives. Finally, it determines how we think and feel about people, places, and things, which affect how we interact with them.

When we have an exclusively ego-centered perspective, it can initiate a pattern that undermines our inner nature. And then we feel the effects. We feel that something is not quite right. So, if life is a test, it might just be about experiencing our inner personal nature while participating in an outer, often impersonal everyday reality.

A final takeaway is that reality is either fully, or to some degree, set before we are born. Some believe it's randomly set, some believe we choose it, and some believe we accept the life *given* to us. Either way, once we are born, *it is the meaning we place on the events* of our life, and actions based on the meaning, that determine our experience of ourselves, our purpose, and our reality.

- Key Insight 18 -
Discovery and Creation

*Great entrepreneurship means experiencing life
as a process of discovery and creation.*

⊶

'Walking our path' is a way of living in the world based on our purpose and personal destiny. One's path is both discovered and created. It is *discovered* because its essence already *exists* - already there for us *to* discover. However, when we walk our path, we also sense we are creating each step as we take it. This is because every step is being created to fulfill an aspect of our inner nature.

So, although we are creating it from our inner source, we feel as though we are discovering it in our outer everyday world. A good metaphor for this process is what happens when we dream. It feels as though things are just happening and we are discovering them along the path of our dream. But the truth is that we are usually creating them moment-by-moment based on what we have been doing, thinking, feeling in our waking life.

So, unlike intuitive dreams where we are accessing higher knowledge, in *this* dream metaphor, our dream is a matrix-like illusory reality, and our waking life is our true reality. And the takeaway here is for us to not only navigate our success map with the joy of discovery, but also with the realization that our success is being created from our higher inner self and our spirit of helping others.

- Key Insight 19 -
Imagination and Manifestation

Great entrepreneurship means practicing the power of imagination and manifestation.

Here is a deeper and more intuitive way to look at two common elements of practical success - *setting goals and achieving goals.* And we'll do this with two five-syllable words: imagination and manifestation.

M*anifestation* has grown in popularity as an idea that is linked to our inner self. As for me, the reason I like the word, *manifestation* more than words like *actualization* is that our purpose and personal destiny are already *actual*, and what happens in everyday reality is simply an expression and reflection of it.

So essentially, what manifestation means here is the inner creation followed by an outer effect. In other words, first we enter our imagination to discover events that are destined to occur in the everyday world. These events begin as something we might more commonly refer to as *action items,* which originate from our *plans, goals, objectives, to-do list,* etc.

To access our imagination, we enter through a door to an inner place in the form of meditation, contemplation, or just some quiet time that provides creative distance between our inner purpose and our outer world.

Once we settle into our meditative or contemplative state, we totally immerse ourselves in the sense of our purpose and personal destiny. With our intention clear, we then receive guidance, which we record. And then we place the items we receive (plans, goals, objectives, action items, etc.) in an order, and we give ourselves to them.

So, we receive and we give. And to put the 'giving of ourselves' aspect in perspective, let's look at some synonyms we might favor: *dedicate and commit,* and all the way to words like *pledge and devote.*

Following this thought, the process is to meditate or take some quiet time and let items emerge that support our purpose and personal destiny. We can begin by saying a statement of purpose, which will open the door for items such as plans, goals, objectives, etc. to emerge from the inner world of our imagination. We then record our items as they arrange themselves into relevant timeframes (hours, days, weeks, months, years).

With our items arranged in time, we then give ourself to them, and observe them manifesting in our everyday reality. And finally, we record relevant outcomes.

Consider that with recording your Keynotes entries, you are *writing a book* that may be more practical and useful to you than any general motivation or success method book. And this is because it is specifically about *you*, *your* life, the people, places, things, and activities of *your* world, as they relate to an important purpose in *your* life.

By learning to see our success in life through the perspective of our keynotes in our notebook/journal/log entries, that derive from our intuition or our inner meditative, we are deepening our experience of life.
And again, if we believe that our inner nature is our most essential nature, then our most essential success in life is *founded* upon our inner nature.

We know we have found our purpose and are fulfilling our personal destiny when we feel that our actions are originating from an intuitive place rather than from common motivations of the timebound framework of the everyday world.

Originating from this intuitive place, we don't have to 'try' to do anything. We let ourself be moved, let ourself be carried by its energy, let ourself be in the flow of our intuitive guidance system. And we find that it all guides our purpose in accordance with our highest regarded values.

- Key Insight 20 -
Our Innermost Being

Great entrepreneurship means being on an inner journey,
and knowing that the path to our innermost being,
is in each eternal moment.

⚿

When we choose to help others, we create a reality aligned to our inner nature, which leads us to our original and innermost being. So, let's take the ultimate deep dive, beginning with the spirit of helping others …

Helping others brings us out of our individual ego,
as we are focusing on 'the other'.

'The other' is represented by other people, other life,
other beings, and finally, the ultimate Other –
our original source - which leads us back
to our essential inner self,
our ultimate innermost being.

So, a mystery remains:
What is our original source?

Whether we think in terms of reality deriving from our consciousness or from the universe, the word *source* refers to that from which our reality originates.

We can't imagine an originating or starting point of reality, because we can always ask what came before that point. Therefore, we conclude that our source must be infinite, which we also can't fathom with our linear, sequential rational minds.

And so, the way might only be found by moving inward, beyond our sequential ego mind, through layers of consciousness, until we arrive at a state and an experience beyond our ego. The front cover of this book represents *the Golden Ratio* aka *the Fibonacci Sequence.* It suggests that reality can move infinitely inward. On our Key Quest, this movement is made by moving beyond the ego with our deeper and ever more refined spirit of helping others.

When we take this path, we sense that our innermost being exists outside of time, but within us somehow. This is why meditation is so useful. With the practice of meditation, it's not so much about reaching an external goal in time. It's mores about reaching a place within us.

And so, the final existential challenge is that our concept of time leads us to believe that our reality is *not* within us, but embedded in the days, weeks, months, and years of our life. But is our time-bound material life actually a reflection of the reality that we hold within us, and that derives from our innermost being? And so, are we the bridge between our innermost source and outer world?

The grand illusion may be that the outer everyday world and its sense of time are real, and we are adapting to its reality. And the ultimate truth may be that our innermost source and we are real, and our innermost *being* is beyond time, existing forever in the eternal moment. And so, we just might find that our innermost being is expressed and reflected in our aspiring toward, and achieving of the meditative experience of the absolute eternal moment - an experience of physical ease, mental clarity, emotional calm resiliency, and a deep inner peace.

- Key Insight 21 -
Peace, Love, and Truth

Great entrepreneurship means aspiring to peace, love, and truth through our purpose, mission, and vision.

⸻ 🗝 ⸻

The three Key Quest values of *commitment to purpose*, *the spirit of helping others*, and *the practice of meditation* can open inner doors to experience peace, love, and truth.

1) With commitment to purpose, we align our *personal* self to our mission and vision, and experience the *peace* of letting go of the concerns of our ego in the process.
2) With the spirit of helping others, we align our *social* self to our mission and vision, and experience *love* as we let go our ego and dedicate ourself to those we are serving with our brand. 3) With the practice of meditation, we align our *inner* self to our mission and vision, and experience the *truth* of our innermost being, and that it has within it the destiny of our human identity and its purpose.

Here is an excerpt from the song, *The Keyholder* that reflects the message of this final *Key Insight* …

In your life are many doors.
Only you know what they're for.
You have found the key to your inner doors.
You will always be the keyholder.
So, open the door to love,
Open the door to truth,
Open the door to peace,
Open the door to you.

Part Nine
Key Qualities

Here in Part Nine, we'll look at Key Qualities that can support your Inner Journey as a compassionate, purpose-centered, and thoughtful entrepreneur, along with the game, *The Inner Marathon*.

A marathon involves *physically* running 26 miles. *The Inner Marathon* involves *mentally* running through 26 *inner* milestones – 26 qualities that follow the letters of the alphabet. When you complete your inner marathon 'rundown', you choose a quality to create your monolog or performance. Or you can spin an online alphabet wheel to find your quality that correlates to your letter.

Here is a script that features the 26 milestone qualities, presented in 'the rundown', followed by a sentence to introduce your monolog/performance in your game activity, or when presenting in *the Key Quest Awards*:

The Inner Marathon Milestone Qualities are:

Self-Acceptance, **B**elief, **C**onfidence, and **D**etermination.
Self-Expression, **F**ulfillment, **G**rowth, and **H**onesty
Self-Image, **J**oy, **K**nowledge, and **L**ove
Self-Management, **N**urturance, **O**bservation, **P**ositivity
Self-Query, **R**ealization. **S**ufficiency, and **T**ranscendence
Self-Understanding. **V**alidation, **W**orth, and **X**-Factor
Self-Yearning and **Self-Z**ealousness

My milestone quality for the moment is self-_____, and here is my monolog/performance.

And here is a little story commemorating the process ...

The Fable of the Inner Marathon

*Once there were two friends
who ran a marathon from beginning to end
by connecting each mile with a special word.
The first was acceptance, the second was belief,
and confidence was the third.*

*And as the words followed the alphabet,
it became a list they would never forget.
So, it was on that day, with that race they ran,
that the game, The Inner Marathon began.*

*And if you want to play the Inner Marathon,
let the 26 qualities run through your mind -
from self-acceptance to self-zealousness.
And choose the one that's most important at this time
for your inner self development.
Then affirm the inner quality and answer the Q's,
and you'll discover a self-clarity that you will never lose.*

So, again, for the developmental process, you can find your quality by perusing (mentally running) through the list and intuitively selecting the quality that would be most valuable to explore at this moment in your life.

Or for the game version, you can search for an *online alphabet wheel*, spin the wheel, and look up the quality that correlates to the landing letter.

Once you choose your quality, or discover it through a spin on the wheel, you take a moment to read your affirmation silently or aloud. Following the affirmation, you will find 10 questions. You can go through them in sequence or you can choose one or more that are most important to you at the moment. Or you can create your own topics. You can also record your answers and ideas in your Keynotes to review. The possible combinations of qualities and questions you answer are in the millions! So, welcome to a universe of self-development!

Reviewing your answers and ideas can reveal:

- how the quality can positively impact your life personally or as an entrepreneur.
- insights about your deeper nature and personality.
- patterns in your life regarding the quality.
- a relationship between the particular quality and your overall self-development.
- how the development of the quality was supported or was possibly hindered in your life.
- who can be effective role models/mentors in your life.
- a path you can take to develop/strengthen the quality.

The ultimate goal is to arrive at some insight or even a revelation about yourself - your personal life, social life, entrepreneurial life, and perhaps most importantly, your inner life. So, an intangible deeper benefit is that it may provide wisdom; and a tangible practical benefit is that it may provide guidance and direction regarding your brand leadership and purpose. And when you make an entry in your keynotes about a benefit or a positive experience or result, you begin a positive cumulative process in which the benefits of the positive quality expand in your life.

An Inner Marathon Bedtime Practice

Here we go from 26 miles to 26 smiles, with a bedtime practice you can do while falling asleep. As you inhale, silently say the word 'self'; and as you exhale, say each quality as you follow the A-to-Z sequence. Feel yourself subtly smiling in a way that connects you to each quality, and you may find yourself waking the next morning in a very positive mindset. And if you take five minutes in your day to go through the affirmations, you may also benefit from having their self-development messages internalizing through the process.

Classification of the 26 Key Qualities

- Among the 26 Key Qualities, you will find those that encourage **self-care**, such as: Self-Acceptance, Self-Belief, Self-Growth, Self-Honesty, Self-Love, Self-Nurturance, Self-Validation, and Self-Worth.
- Then there are those related to your **self-presentation**, such as: Self Confidence, Self-Expression, Self-Image.
- There are qualities that recognize your **individual unique nature**, such as Self-Knowledge, Self-Realization, Self-Understanding, and Self-X-Factor.
- Then there are those that are directly related to **success**, such as: Self-Determination Self-Fulfillment, Self-Management, and Self-Observation.
- There are those **optimal states** of Self-Joy, Self-Positivity, Self-Sufficiency, and Self-Zealousness.
- And finally, since this is an inner journey, you will find those **sublime inner qualities** found in Self-Query, Self-Transcendence, and Self-Yearning.

The Inner Marathon

NAME
The name, *The Inner Marathon* refers to the 26 miles of a physical marathon translated to an inner marathon and 26 inner milestone qualities that support personal, social, entrepreneurial, and inner development.

FRAME
The frame of *The Inner Marathon* is that of a self-selection or online alphabet wheel game, in which 26 key qualities follow the 26 letters of the alphabet. The play involves selecting your quality, or discovering your letter on your wheel spin and finding the correlating quality. Next, you make/consider your affirmation, and then do a monolog or performance, opting to use one or more of the 10 questions that follow the affirmation for motivation. The idea is to present your monolog or performance in a way that expresses your own feelings about the quality, and inspires others on *their* journey regarding the value of the quality. Winners can be selected by the *place they finish in the marathon*. And as with all the Key Quest games and game activities, you can also choose to participate in *the Key Quest Awards* in which performers compete within a larger platform.

AIM
The aim of *The Inner Marathon game activities* is to get in touch with your personal, social, entrepreneurial, and inner nature. Of course, the game can be played solo, with friends, family, associates, and/or with as many people who are interested in playing and/or performing!

SELF
ACCEPTANCE

I am comfortable being me.

I experience a sense of ease and inner calm that expresses and reflects my contentment with who I am.

I am happy with who I am.

1. Why is this quality valuable to you as an entrepreneur?
2. How can you practice, express, exhibit, or role-model this quality as an entrepreneur?
3. How can you practice, express, exhibit, or role-model this quality in another area (personal life, social life, etc.)?
4. Who in the world today represents this quality and inspires you? How can you emulate them?
5. What is a significant memory of how you experienced this quality? What was the situation or circumstances? What can you learn from that memory to have more of the quality in your life?
6. What is a significant memory of not experiencing this quality? What was the situation or circumstances? What can you learn from that memory to have more of the quality in your life?
7. Who was a good adult role model of this quality in your childhood years (someone who exhibited it)?
8. Who was not a good adult role model of this quality in your childhood years (someone who didn't exhibit it)?
9. Who supported you in experiencing this quality?
10. Who did not support you in experiencing this quality?

For Questions 7 through 10: Reflect on the person and create something positive/valuable for yourself regarding this quality.

SELF
BELIEF

I believe in myself.

**I know that people will believe in me when I first believe in myself.
I believe in my ideas and my dreams.**

I believe in who I am, and what I represent.

1. Why is this quality valuable to you as an entrepreneur?
2. How can you practice, express, exhibit, or role-model this quality as an entrepreneur?
3. How can you practice, express, exhibit, or role-model this quality in another area (personal life, social life, etc.)?
4. Who in the world today represents this quality and inspires you? How can you emulate them?
5. What is a significant memory of how you experienced this quality? What was the situation or circumstances? What can you learn from that memory to have more of the quality in your life?
6. What is a significant memory of not experiencing this quality? What was the situation or circumstances? What can you learn from that memory to have more of the quality in your life?
7. Who was a good adult role model of this quality in your childhood years (someone who exhibited it)?
8. Who was not a good adult role model of this quality in your childhood years (someone who didn't exhibit it)?
9. Who supported you in experiencing this quality?
10. Who did not support you in experiencing this quality?

For Questions 7 through 10: Reflect on the person and create something positive/valuable for yourself regarding this quality.

SELF
CONFIDENCE

I have confidence in myself.

I trust in my judgement, my decisions, my talents and my abilities, and my traits and skills.

My confidence supports my poise and inner calm.

1. Why is this quality valuable to you as an entrepreneur?
2. How can you practice, express, exhibit, or role-model this quality as an entrepreneur?
3. How can you practice, express, exhibit, or role-model this quality in another area (personal life, social life, etc.)?
4. Who in the world today represents this quality and inspires you? How can you emulate them?
5. What is a significant memory of how you experienced this quality? What was the situation or circumstances? What can you learn from that memory to have more of the quality in your life?
6. What is a significant memory of not experiencing this quality? What was the situation or circumstances? What can you learn from that memory to have more of the quality in your life?
7. Who was a good adult role model of this quality in your childhood years (someone who exhibited it)?
8. Who was not a good adult role model of this quality in your childhood years (someone who didn't exhibit it)?
9. Who supported you in experiencing this quality?
10. Who did not support you in experiencing this quality?

For Questions 7 through 10: Reflect on the person and create something positive/valuable for yourself regarding this quality.

SELF
DETERMINATION

I am taking charge of my life.

I am setting personally meaningful goals, being realistic about my strengths and weaknesses, and making choices that assure that I achieve my goals.

I am staying focused and staying true to myself.

1. Why is this quality valuable to you as an entrepreneur?
2. How can you practice, express, exhibit, or role-model this quality as an entrepreneur?
3. How can you practice, express, exhibit, or role-model this quality in another area (personal life, social life, etc.)?
4. Who in the world today represents this quality and inspires you? How can you emulate them?
5. What is a significant memory of how you experienced this quality? What was the situation or circumstances? What can you learn from that memory to have more of the quality in your life?
6. What is a significant memory of not experiencing this quality? What was the situation or circumstances? What can you learn from that memory to have more of the quality in your life?
7. Who was a good adult role model of this quality in your childhood years (someone who exhibited it)?
8. Who was not a good adult role model of this quality in your childhood years (someone who didn't exhibit it)?
9. Who supported you in experiencing this quality?
10. Who did not support you in experiencing this quality?

For Questions 7 through 10: Reflect on the person and create something positive/valuable for yourself regarding this quality.

SELF
EXPRESSION

I express myself naturally without worry or regret.

**I am comfortable with how I express myself
in words, facial expression, and body language.
I enjoy expressing my unique nature.**

I also enjoy the ways that others express themselves.

1. Why is this quality valuable to you as an entrepreneur?
2. How can you practice, express, exhibit, or role-model this quality as an entrepreneur?
3. How can you practice, express, exhibit, or role-model this quality in another area (personal life, social life, etc.)?
4. Who in the world today represents this quality and inspires you? How can you emulate them?
5. What is a significant memory of how you experienced this quality? What was the situation or circumstances? What can you learn from that memory to have more of the quality in your life?
6. What is a significant memory of not experiencing this quality? What was the situation or circumstances? What can you learn from that memory to have more of the quality in your life?
7. Who was a good adult role model of this quality in your childhood years (someone who exhibited it)?
8. Who was not a good adult role model of this quality in your childhood years (someone who didn't exhibit it)?
9. Who supported you in experiencing this quality?
10. Who did not support you in experiencing this quality?

For Questions 7 through 10: Reflect on the person
and create something positive/valuable for yourself regarding this quality.

SELF
FULFILLMENT

Self-fulfillment begins with my inner self.

I am striving to express my *true* best inner self in the choices I make and actions I take in life. In this way, my inner self is fulfilled in the simple act of living.

So, my authenticity supports my self-fulfillment.

1. Why is this quality valuable to you as an entrepreneur?
2. How can you practice, express, exhibit, or role-model this quality as an entrepreneur?
3. How can you practice, express, exhibit, or role-model this quality in another area (personal life, social life, etc.)?
4. Who in the world today represents this quality and inspires you? How can you emulate them?
5. What is a significant memory of how you experienced this quality? What was the situation or circumstances? What can you learn from that memory to have more of the quality in your life?
6. What is a significant memory of not experiencing this quality? What was the situation or circumstances? What can you learn from that memory to have more of the quality in your life?
7. Who was a good adult role model of this quality in your childhood years (someone who exhibited it)?
8. Who was not a good adult role model of this quality in your childhood years (someone who didn't exhibit it)?
9. Who supported you in experiencing this quality?
10. Who did not support you in experiencing this quality?

For Questions 7 through 10: Reflect on the person and create something positive/valuable for yourself regarding this quality.

SELF
GROWTH

Every day I am growing in my knowledge and skills.

I see my choices, actions and encounters as opportunities for growth, development, and positive change.

Every day I experience positive personal growth.

1. Why is this quality valuable to you as an entrepreneur?
2. How can you practice, express, exhibit, or role-model this quality as an entrepreneur?
3. How can you practice, express, exhibit, or role-model this quality in another area (personal life, social life, etc.)?
4. Who in the world today represents this quality and inspires you? How can you emulate them?
5. What is a significant memory of how you experienced this quality? What was the situation or circumstances? What can you learn from that memory to have more of the quality in your life?
6. What is a significant memory of not experiencing this quality? What was the situation or circumstances? What can you learn from that memory to have more of the quality in your life?
7. Who was a good adult role model of this quality in your childhood years (someone who exhibited it)?
8. Who was not a good adult role model of this quality in your childhood years (someone who didn't exhibit it)?
9. Who supported you in experiencing this quality?
10. Who did not support you in experiencing this quality?

For Questions 7 through 10: Reflect on the person and create something positive/valuable for yourself regarding this quality.

SELF
HONESTY

I am becoming more honest with myself.

With my self-honesty, my life is becoming more satisfying, empowering, and peaceful, and less dependent on others.

A friend is honest. I am being a friend to myself.

1. Why is this quality valuable to you as an entrepreneur?
2. How can you practice, express, exhibit, or role-model this quality as an entrepreneur?
3. How can you practice, express, exhibit, or role-model this quality in another area (personal life, social life, etc.)?
4. Who in the world today represents this quality and inspires you? How can you emulate them?
5. What is a significant memory of how you experienced this quality? What was the situation or circumstances? What can you learn from that memory to have more of the quality in your life?
6. What is a significant memory of not experiencing this quality? What was the situation or circumstances? What can you learn from that memory to have more of the quality in your life?
7. Who was a good adult role model of this quality in your childhood years (someone who exhibited it)?
8. Who was not a good adult role model of this quality in your childhood years (someone who didn't exhibit it)?
9. Who supported you in experiencing this quality?
10. Who did not support you in experiencing this quality?

For Questions 7 through 10: Reflect on the person and create something positive/valuable for yourself regarding this quality.

SELF
IMAGE

My self-image impacts the quality of my life.

**People who like me like the person
I see in the mirror every day.
They have a positive image of me.**

I am feeling and thinking positively about myself.

1. Why is this quality valuable to you as an entrepreneur?
2. How can you practice, express, exhibit, or role-model this quality as an entrepreneur?
3. How can you practice, express, exhibit, or role-model this quality in another area (personal life, social life, etc.)?
4. Who in the world today represents this quality and inspires you? How can you emulate them?
5. What is a significant memory of how you experienced this quality? What was the situation or circumstances? What can you learn from that memory to have more of the quality in your life?
6. What is a significant memory of not experiencing this quality? What was the situation or circumstances? What can you learn from that memory to have more of the quality in your life?
7. Who was a good adult role model of this quality in your childhood years (someone who exhibited it)?
8. Who was not a good adult role model of this quality in your childhood years (someone who didn't exhibit it)?
9. Who supported you in experiencing this quality?
10. Who did not support you in experiencing this quality?

For Questions 7 through 10: Reflect on the person and create something positive/valuable for yourself regarding this quality.

SELF
JOY

I experience moments of joy in just being alive.

These are the moments when I feel like I am in the flow of life, doing what I am meant to be doing, and being exactly the person I am meant to be.

I am experiencing the joy of simply being me.

1. Why is this quality valuable to you as an entrepreneur?
2. How can you practice, express, exhibit, or role-model this quality as an entrepreneur?
3. How can you practice, express, exhibit, or role-model this quality in another area (personal life, social life, etc.)?
4. Who in the world today represents this quality and inspires you? How can you emulate them?
5. What is a significant memory of how you experienced this quality? What was the situation or circumstances? What can you learn from that memory to have more of the quality in your life?
6. What is a significant memory of not experiencing this quality? What was the situation or circumstances? What can you learn from that memory to have more of the quality in your life?
7. Who was a good adult role model of this quality in your childhood years (someone who exhibited it)?
8. Who was not a good adult role model of this quality in your childhood years (someone who didn't exhibit it)?
9. Who supported you in experiencing this quality?
10. Who did not support you in experiencing this quality?

For Questions 7 through 10: Reflect on the person and create something positive/valuable for yourself regarding this quality.

SELF
KNOWLEDGE

I am getting to know the real me.

With my self-knowledge, I am being more honest with myself, and more sincere in my relationships.

I am discovering what really matters to me.

1. Why is this quality valuable to you as an entrepreneur?
2. How can you practice, express, exhibit, or role-model this quality as an entrepreneur?
3. How can you practice, express, exhibit, or role-model this quality in another area (personal life, social life, etc.)?
4. Who in the world today represents this quality and inspires you? How can you emulate them?
5. What is a significant memory of how you experienced this quality? What was the situation or circumstances? What can you learn from that memory to have more of the quality in your life?
6. What is a significant memory of not experiencing this quality? What was the situation or circumstances? What can you learn from that memory to have more of the quality in your life?
7. Who was a good adult role model of this quality in your childhood years (someone who exhibited it)?
8. Who was not a good adult role model of this quality in your childhood years (someone who didn't exhibit it)?
9. Who supported you in experiencing this quality?
10. Who did not support you in experiencing this quality?

For Questions 7 through 10: Reflect on the person and create something positive/valuable for yourself regarding this quality.

SELF
LOVE

I know the deep importance of loving oneself.

Love for others, love for the planet, and the highest love I can experience all begin with loving this person that I am.

And so, I am feeling love and compassion for myself.

1. Why is this quality valuable to you as an entrepreneur?
2. How can you practice, express, exhibit, or role-model this quality as an entrepreneur?
3. How can you practice, express, exhibit, or role-model this quality in another area (personal life, social life, etc.)?
4. Who in the world today represents this quality and inspires you? How can you emulate them?
5. What is a significant memory of how you experienced this quality? What was the situation or circumstances? What can you learn from that memory to have more of the quality in your life?
6. What is a significant memory of not experiencing this quality? What was the situation or circumstances? What can you learn from that memory to have more of the quality in your life?
7. Who was a good adult role model of this quality in your childhood years (someone who exhibited it)?
8. Who was not a good adult role model of this quality in your childhood years (someone who didn't exhibit it)?
9. Who supported you in experiencing this quality?
10. Who did not support you in experiencing this quality?

For Questions 7 through 10: Reflect on the person and create something positive/valuable for yourself regarding this quality.

SELF
MANAGEMENT

I know how very important self-management is.

Every day I am learning to better manage my behavior, my thoughts, and my feelings for personal satisfaction and social well-being.

I can restore my inner calm whenever I want.

1. Why is this quality valuable to you as an entrepreneur?
2. How can you practice, express, exhibit, or role-model this quality as an entrepreneur?
3. How can you practice, express, exhibit, or role-model this quality in another area (personal life, social life, etc.)?
4. Who in the world today represents this quality and inspires you? How can you emulate them?
5. What is a significant memory of how you experienced this quality? What was the situation or circumstances? What can you learn from that memory to have more of the quality in your life?
6. What is a significant memory of not experiencing this quality? What was the situation or circumstances? What can you learn from that memory to have more of the quality in your life?
7. Who was a good adult role model of this quality in your childhood years (someone who exhibited it)?
8. Who was not a good adult role model of this quality in your childhood years (someone who didn't exhibit it)?
9. Who supported you in experiencing this quality?
10. Who did not support you in experiencing this quality?

For Questions 7 through 10: Reflect on the person and create something positive/valuable for yourself regarding this quality.

SELF
NURTURANCE

I am aware of how important health is in one's life.

I am sensitive to those things that can affect my own health, both positive and negative, and I am making choices that nurture my mind, body, and spirit.

I aspire to wellness in mind, body, and spirit.

1. Why is this quality valuable to you as an entrepreneur?
2. How can you practice, express, exhibit, or role-model this quality as an entrepreneur?
3. How can you practice, express, exhibit, or role-model this quality in another area (personal life, social life, etc.)?
4. Who in the world today represents this quality and inspires you? How can you emulate them?
5. What is a significant memory of how you experienced this quality? What was the situation or circumstances? What can you learn from that memory to have more of the quality in your life?
6. What is a significant memory of not experiencing this quality? What was the situation or circumstances? What can you learn from that memory to have more of the quality in your life?
7. Who was a good adult role model of this quality in your childhood years (someone who exhibited it)?
8. Who was not a good adult role model of this quality in your childhood years (someone who didn't exhibit it)?
9. Who supported you in experiencing this quality?
10. Who did not support you in experiencing this quality?

For Questions 7 through 10: Reflect on the person and create something positive/valuable for yourself regarding this quality.

SELF
OBSERVATION

I am making time for some self-observation.

When I want to make a change, improve an area, refine a skill, etc., I observe my current actions and behaviors regarding the area or skill.

By observing myself, I then know how to proceed.

1. Why is this quality valuable to you as an entrepreneur?
2. How can you practice, express, exhibit, or role-model this quality as an entrepreneur?
3. How can you practice, express, exhibit, or role-model this quality in another area (personal life, social life, etc.)?
4. Who in the world today represents this quality and inspires you? How can you emulate them?
5. What is a significant memory of how you experienced this quality? What was the situation or circumstances? What can you learn from that memory to have more of the quality in your life?
6. What is a significant memory of not experiencing this quality? What was the situation or circumstances? What can you learn from that memory to have more of the quality in your life?
7. Who was a good adult role model of this quality in your childhood years (someone who exhibited it)?
8. Who was not a good adult role model of this quality in your childhood years (someone who didn't exhibit it)?
9. Who supported you in experiencing this quality?
10. Who did not support you in experiencing this quality?

For Questions 7 through 10: Reflect on the person
and create something positive/valuable for yourself regarding this quality.

SELF
POSITIVITY

I aspire to be positive in all areas of my life.

**When I have a negative thought,
I look for a way to turn it around
and make it into a positive thought or feeling.**

I associate with positive people, places, and things.

1. Why is this quality valuable to you as an entrepreneur?
2. How can you practice, express, exhibit, or role-model this quality as an entrepreneur?
3. How can you practice, express, exhibit, or role-model this quality in another area (personal life, social life, etc.)?
4. Who in the world today represents this quality and inspires you? How can you emulate them?
5. What is a significant memory of how you experienced this quality? What was the situation or circumstances? What can you learn from that memory to have more of the quality in your life?
6. What is a significant memory of not experiencing this quality? What was the situation or circumstances? What can you learn from that memory to have more of the quality in your life?
7. Who was a good adult role model of this quality in your childhood years (someone who exhibited it)?
8. Who was not a good adult role model of this quality in your childhood years (someone who didn't exhibit it)?
9. Who supported you in experiencing this quality?
10. Who did not support you in experiencing this quality?

For Questions 7 through 10: Reflect on the person
and create something positive/valuable for yourself regarding this quality.

SELF
QUERY

I aspire to know my innermost or higher self.

I take time to get in touch with this essential part of myself by asking the big questions like, "Who am I?" "Why am I here?" and "What is my purpose?"

In this way, I live my life with more clarity and peace.

1. Why is this quality valuable to you as an entrepreneur?
2. How can you practice, express, exhibit, or role-model this quality as an entrepreneur?
3. How can you practice, express, exhibit, or role-model this quality in another area (personal life, social life, etc.)?
4. Who in the world today represents this quality and inspires you? How can you emulate them?
5. What is a significant memory of how you experienced this quality? What was the situation or circumstances? What can you learn from that memory to have more of the quality in your life?
6. What is a significant memory of not experiencing this quality? What was the situation or circumstances? What can you learn from that memory to have more of the quality in your life?
7. Who was a good adult role model of this quality in your childhood years (someone who exhibited it)?
8. Who was not a good adult role model of this quality in your childhood years (someone who didn't exhibit it)?
9. Who supported you in experiencing this quality?
10. Who did not support you in experiencing this quality?

For Questions 7 through 10: Reflect on the person and create something positive/valuable for yourself regarding this quality.

SELF
REALIZATION

Realization begins with the word, *real*.

I am becoming more real, authentic, genuine and transparent, as I am realizing and accepting my own inner nature and sharing it with others.

More and more, I am learning to live authentically.

1. Why is this quality valuable to you as an entrepreneur?
2. How can you practice, express, exhibit, or role-model this quality as an entrepreneur?
3. How can you practice, express, exhibit, or role-model this quality in another area (personal life, social life, etc.)?
4. Who in the world today represents this quality and inspires you? How can you emulate them?
5. What is a significant memory of how you experienced this quality? What was the situation or circumstances? What can you learn from that memory to have more of the quality in your life?
6. What is a significant memory of not experiencing this quality? What was the situation or circumstances? What can you learn from that memory to have more of the quality in your life?
7. Who was a good adult role model of this quality in your childhood years (someone who exhibited it)?
8. Who was not a good adult role model of this quality in your childhood years (someone who didn't exhibit it)?
9. Who supported you in experiencing this quality?
10. Who did not support you in experiencing this quality?

For Questions 7 through 10: Reflect on the person and create something positive/valuable for yourself regarding this quality.

SELF
SUFFICIENCY

I feel complete within myself.

Although I have both material goals and goals for my development, I experience life in a way that provides me with an ongoing innate sense of self-sufficiency.

I feel at home within myself.

1. Why is this quality valuable to you as an entrepreneur?
2. How can you practice, express, exhibit, or role-model this quality as an entrepreneur?
3. How can you practice, express, exhibit, or role-model this quality in another area (personal life, social life, etc.)?
4. Who in the world today represents this quality and inspires you? How can you emulate them?
5. What is a significant memory of how you experienced this quality? What was the situation or circumstances? What can you learn from that memory to have more of the quality in your life?
6. What is a significant memory of not experiencing this quality? What was the situation or circumstances? What can you learn from that memory to have more of the quality in your life?
7. Who was a good adult role model of this quality in your childhood years (someone who exhibited it)?
8. Who was not a good adult role model of this quality in your childhood years (someone who didn't exhibit it)?
9. Who supported you in experiencing this quality?
10. Who did not support you in experiencing this quality?

For Questions 7 through 10: Reflect on the person and create something positive/valuable for yourself regarding this quality.

SELF
TRANSCENDANCE

I am learning to experience something greater in life.

I am learning to transcend my own needs and desires of the moment, and focus on my purpose, mission, higher values, and helping others.

I am experiencing a blend of wonder and peace.

1. Why is this quality valuable to you as an entrepreneur?
2. How can you practice, express, exhibit, or role-model this quality as an entrepreneur?
3. How can you practice, express, exhibit, or role-model this quality in another area (personal life, social life, etc.)?
4. Who in the world today represents this quality and inspires you? How can you emulate them?
5. What is a significant memory of how you experienced this quality? What was the situation or circumstances? What can you learn from that memory to have more of the quality in your life?
6. What is a significant memory of not experiencing this quality? What was the situation or circumstances? What can you learn from that memory to have more of the quality in your life?
7. Who was a good adult role model of this quality in your childhood years (someone who exhibited it)?
8. Who was not a good adult role model of this quality in your childhood years (someone who didn't exhibit it)?
9. Who supported you in experiencing this quality?
10. Who did not support you in experiencing this quality?

For Questions 7 through 10: Reflect on the person and create something positive/valuable for yourself regarding this quality.

SELF
UNDERSTANDING

Self-understanding is bringing clarity to my life.

Understanding more about who I am inside is making me more objective and realistic about my strengths and my challenges.

With this wisdom, I also better understand others.

1. Why is this quality valuable to you as an entrepreneur?
2. How can you practice, express, exhibit, or role-model this quality as an entrepreneur?
3. How can you practice, express, exhibit, or role-model this quality in another area (personal life, social life, etc.)?
4. Who in the world today represents this quality and inspires you? How can you emulate them?
5. What is a significant memory of how you experienced this quality? What was the situation or circumstances? What can you learn from that memory to have more of the quality in your life?
6. What is a significant memory of not experiencing this quality? What was the situation or circumstances? What can you learn from that memory to have more of the quality in your life?
7. Who was a good adult role model of this quality in your childhood years (someone who exhibited it)?
8. Who was not a good adult role model of this quality in your childhood years (someone who didn't exhibit it)?
9. Who supported you in experiencing this quality?
10. Who did not support you in experiencing this quality?

For Questions 7 through 10: Reflect on the person and create something positive/valuable for yourself regarding this quality.

SELF
VALIDATION

I don't judge myself harshly or negatively.

As 'validation' means accepting the feelings and thoughts of others, self-validation means accepting my own feelings and thoughts.

As I *accept* myself, I also strive to *better* myself.

1. Why is this quality valuable to you as an entrepreneur?
2. How can you practice, express, exhibit, or role-model this quality as an entrepreneur?
3. How can you practice, express, exhibit, or role-model this quality in another area (personal life, social life, etc.)?
4. Who in the world today represents this quality and inspires you? How can you emulate them?
5. What is a significant memory of how you experienced this quality? What was the situation or circumstances? What can you learn from that memory to have more of the quality in your life?
6. What is a significant memory of not experiencing this quality? What was the situation or circumstances? What can you learn from that memory to have more of the quality in your life?
7. Who was a good adult role model of this quality in your childhood years (someone who exhibited it)?
8. Who was not a good adult role model of this quality in your childhood years (someone who didn't exhibit it)?
9. Who supported you in experiencing this quality?
10. Who did not support you in experiencing this quality?

For Questions 7 through 10: Reflect on the person and create something positive/valuable for yourself regarding this quality.

SELF
WORTH

Self-worth is an internal sense of being worthy.

My self-worth is defined by my deepest genuine positive values about myself, and the meaning of life as I experience it.

I am worthy of acceptance, success, and love.

1. Why is this quality valuable to you as an entrepreneur?
2. How can you practice, express, exhibit, or role-model this quality as an entrepreneur?
3. How can you practice, express, exhibit, or role-model this quality in another area (personal life, social life, etc.)?
4. Who in the world today represents this quality and inspires you? How can you emulate them?
5. What is a significant memory of how you experienced this quality? What was the situation or circumstances? What can you learn from that memory to have more of the quality in your life?
6. What is a significant memory of not experiencing this quality? What was the situation or circumstances? What can you learn from that memory to have more of the quality in your life?
7. Who was a good adult role model of this quality in your childhood years (someone who exhibited it)?
8. Who was not a good adult role model of this quality in your childhood years (someone who didn't exhibit it)?
9. Who supported you in experiencing this quality?
10. Who did not support you in experiencing this quality?

For Questions 7 through 10: Reflect on the person and create something positive/valuable for yourself regarding this quality.

SELF
X-FACTOR

Everyone has a personal X-Factor, so I have one too.

I am looking at what it is about me that contributes to my personal X-Factor, and how it can create positive situations, relationships, and results.

I am getting comfortable with my personal X-Factor.

1. Why is this quality valuable to you as an entrepreneur?
2. How can you practice, express, exhibit, or role-model this quality as an entrepreneur?
3. How can you practice, express, exhibit, or role-model this quality in another area (personal life, social life, etc.)?
4. Who in the world today represents this quality and inspires you? How can you emulate them?
5. What is a significant memory of how you experienced this quality? What was the situation or circumstances? What can you learn from that memory to have more of the quality in your life?
6. What is a significant memory of not experiencing this quality? What was the situation or circumstances? What can you learn from that memory to have more of the quality in your life?
7. Who was a good adult role model of this quality in your childhood years (someone who exhibited it)?
8. Who was not a good adult role model of this quality in your childhood years (someone who didn't exhibit it)?
9. Who supported you in experiencing this quality?
10. Who did not support you in experiencing this quality?

For Questions 7 through 10: Reflect on the person and create something positive/valuable for yourself regarding this quality.

SELF
YEARNING

I have moments of intuitive self-yearning.

I sometimes feel there is something more to my life, something profound and beyond the appearances of the everyday world, beyond all human concerns.

I accept these moments with wonder and gratitude.

1. Why is this quality valuable to you as an entrepreneur?
2. How can you practice, express, exhibit, or role-model this quality as an entrepreneur?
3. How can you practice, express, exhibit, or role-model this quality in another area (personal life, social life, etc.)?
4. Who in the world today represents this quality and inspires you? How can you emulate them?
5. What is a significant memory of how you experienced this quality? What was the situation or circumstances? What can you learn from that memory to have more of the quality in your life?
6. What is a significant memory of not experiencing this quality? What was the situation or circumstances? What can you learn from that memory to have more of the quality in your life?
7. Who was a good adult role model of this quality in your childhood years (someone who exhibited it)?
8. Who was not a good adult role model of this quality in your childhood years (someone who didn't exhibit it)?
9. Who supported you in experiencing this quality?
10. Who did not support you in experiencing this quality?

For Questions 7 through 10: Reflect on the person and create something positive/valuable for yourself regarding this quality.

SELF
ZEALOUSNESS

I am zealous about my life, and its value to others.

**Synonyms for zealousness include passion, dedication, and enthusiasm.
I am dedicated, passionate, and enthusiastic.**

I bring these qualities to myself, and to help others.

1. Why is this quality valuable to you as an entrepreneur?
2. How can you practice, express, exhibit, or role-model this quality as an entrepreneur?
3. How can you practice, express, exhibit, or role-model this quality in another area (personal life, social life, etc.)?
4. Who in the world today represents this quality and inspires you? How can you emulate them?
5. What is a significant memory of how you experienced this quality? What was the situation or circumstances? What can you learn from that memory to have more of the quality in your life?
6. What is a significant memory of not experiencing this quality? What was the situation or circumstances? What can you learn from that memory to have more of the quality in your life?
7. Who was a good adult role model of this quality in your childhood years (someone who exhibited it)?
8. Who was not a good adult role model of this quality in your childhood years (someone who didn't exhibit it)?
9. Who supported you in experiencing this quality?
10. Who did not support you in experiencing this quality?

For Questions 7 through 10: Reflect on the person and create something positive/valuable for yourself regarding this quality.

Part Ten
The Inner Journey of the Entrepreneur

The Hero's Journey is a theme that we find repeating throughout history. It was formalized by mythologist, Joseph Campbell as *the monomyth*. This celebrated scholar envisioned 12 steps in the hero's journey. His vision and methodology have been used in popular movies, including Harry Potter and the Philosopher's Stone, Star Wars, The Matrix, Spider-Man, The Lion King, and The Lord of the Rings trilogy.

We can find various versions of the mythology presenting different numbers of steps, from five to 17. With the compassionate, purpose-centered entrepreneur being a crusader for social causes, we can easily see the correlation between the Hero's Journey and the Key Quest, or the Inner Journey of the Entrepreneur.

First, let's dive into the mythology and review seven essential steps of the traditional hero's journey:

1. Living in the ordinary world.
2. Crossing the threshold.
3. Embarking on a journey that includes tests, allies, and adversaries. (Driving forces and restraining forces.)
4. Entering the abyss.
5. Revelations and supernatural guidance.
6. Transformation.
7. The new reality. Returning to the ordinary world with what the hero has found or discovered.

And following are the seven correlating Key Steps of the Key Quest – The Inner Journey of the Entrepreneur.

1. The Outer World and Inner Practice
2. Inner Practice and Purpose
3. Commitment to Purpose
4. Transcending the Ego
5. Inner Guidance
6. The Inner Self
7. Inner Life

The First Key Step: The Outer World and Inner Practice

Our First Key Step correlates to the Hero's Journey step of 'living in the ordinary world'. On that note, let's begin by considering that we start out in life as everyone does - being conditioned by the ideas and beliefs of family, community, society, and our world. And so, we begin our life journey with some baggage, and some of the baggage can be quite negative. As we are destined to become a compassionate and purpose-centered entrepreneur, we discover there is another way besides following the ideas and beliefs of the past. And so, we find a path beyond any obsolete ideas, so that we can move toward a positive future for ourselves and the planet.

And that path involves going beyond the appearances of the outer everyday reality to the truth of our own inner nature. So, we begin an inner practice such as meditation. And with it, we cross from our outer everyday way of thinking to a new inner world of intuition and insight.

The Second Key Step: Inner Practice and Purpose

Our Second Key Step correlates to the Hero's Journey step of 'crossing the threshold'. So, now, within the intuitive nature of our inner practice, we discover a true purpose for our life. We realize that this new direction in life will open us to an adventure that will take us far out of our comfort zone and challenge us personally and socially and in ways that will demand that we reach deep into our innermost nature and access our ultimate resolve and tenacity. With this deep realization, and knowing the ramifications, we take the step into our new world and leave our old familiar world behind. The moment we take this step in the direction of our purpose, we are met with forces, both internal and external, that seem to block our path and fortify the boundary we are seeking to cross.

We have internal thoughts and feelings in the form of worries about what the future might bring, or about leaving behind our familiar life. And then we have the external exposures to people and ideas that can make us feel less sure and certain of our decision to move forward. Finally, we make our move and we begin our life of purpose.

The Third Key Step: Commitment to Purpose

Our Third Key Step correlates to the Hero's Journey step of 'embarking on the journey that includes tests, allies, and adversaries'. And so, we commit to our purpose and experience the joy, the empowerment, the personal satisfaction, along with the challenges and obstacles we find on the way. We travel through stages and levels of achievement and develop our talents and hone our skills.

We become purpose-centered as we dedicate ourselves to the success of our campaign, brand, our purpose, our company. We learn to bring our mission's message into the world as we pass through four rings of positive influence to our innermost place of truth and calm. We develop competencies that are essential to the life of an entrepreneur, such as organization, time-management, communication skills, etc. We dive into all those topics relevant to the entrepreneur's journey, such as marketing, the customer journey, supply chain management, and so on. In the process, a strong sense of self develops and strengthens as our entrepreneurial success grows and our status is elevated. We are becoming set in our identity, and our ego can also strengthen in the process.

The Fourth Key Step: Transcending the Ego

So, we grow our brand in the outer everyday world and experience success; and along with it, an unintended growing sense of ego. Our ego grows without our realizing it, and we become more self-oriented, and possibly self-centered. Our new state is fed by our exposures to certain subtle messages from our media and other sources that being self-centered is a good and natural thing. Then at some point, we sense that this way of thinking is leading us to develop negative ego traits. If we are truly destined to continue on the hero's journey, we feel that we have to go beyond this lure of power and success. And so, we dedicate ourselves to transcending our ego through developing an even deeper and truer spirit of helping others. And when we finally do, we find ourselves in unfamiliar territory with no ground on which to stand. We encounter a chasm, a void within ourselves – an abyss.

The Fifth Key Step: Inner Guidance

Having transcended the needs of the ego, we are no longer controlled by thoughts and feelings that can entrap us. So, more mental and emotional energy is channeled to support our higher functioning. Breaking the bonds of the outer world's influence, we discover that there is an inner source of counsel and guidance at our disposal that can help us find our way through caverns of doubt, through the abyss, and into the light of our true hero self. All we have to do is tap into this source. As we tap into it with inner practice, idea mining, and receptivity, we discover our inherent wisdom in the form of insights and revelations that guide our decisions and clear our path for entrepreneurial success. And suddenly we feel very natural, genuine, real, authentic. Its impact on our entrepreneurial journey is that we become fully transparent and gain the trust of others.

The Sixth Key Step: The Inner Self

Our new capacity for wisdom, insights, and revelations transforms us as we get more and more in touch with our inner self; and we identify ourselves as such. We find personal and social qualities naturally developing and strengthening within us. Personal qualities such as patience, awareness, composure, and equanimity. Social qualities and values such as compassion, acknowledgement, respect, and encouragement.

With our personal qualities, we pace ourselves in a new calm empowering way. And with our social qualities, we care for others in a genuine and authentic way.

The Seventh Key Step: Inner Life

As we express our inner nature in our outer everyday reality, we find that the world responds to us in like. Somehow the world seems to adapt and adjust itself to complement our positive personal and social qualities, and support our purpose of genuinely helping others with our product, service, content, or brand. And then we realize the profound secret that *the world actually reflects us*. And this leads us to experience our life as an act of creativity. And finally, with our pure creativity, we discover the power of living a life filled with meaning and purpose and truth.

The Inner Journey of the Entrepreneur as a Process and as a Game

As with all of the content of Key Quest, the Inner Journey of the Entrepreneur can be used as a process or played as a game. As a process, read through the questions on the game chart pages in sequence, and record your answers in your Keynotes. Review your notes and add to them to expand your understanding of your life and the place that your purpose and brand has in it.

If you prefer to be entertained with the game version of the content, the next page will walk you through the game, *The Hero's Journey* - the meaning in its name, its structure or frame, and its object or aim.

The Hero's Journey

NAME

The name, *The Hero's Journey* reflects the idea that today's compassionate and purpose-centered entrepreneur is someone who is dedicated to helping others and to making the world a better place – a hero for our time.

FRAME

The frame of *The Hero's Journey* is that of a card game in which the cards' values from Ace through King represent steps and stages in the hero's journey mythology, and are translated to the inner journey of the entrepreneur.

The play involves selecting a card value from Ace to King by: thinking of the card, picking a card from a deck, or using an online *playing card randomizer*. The card can be any one of the four suits. Once selected, you read and answer the questions correlating to the card *value*.

AIM

The aim of *The Hero's Journey* is to get in touch with your inner journey as an entrepreneur - from your back story to your current situation to your future plans. Clarifying who you are and what you stand for in this way can help you to share your personal story and entrepreneurial journey in various activities that support your brand, such as appearing on someone's podcast, for example.

Of course, the game can be played solo, with friends, family, associates, partners, or anyone interested in an entrepreneurial game that supports you or all who are playing.

The Hero's Journey Card Values A - 4

A	In your elementary through middle school years, what ideas or beliefs were you exposed to that could be supportive to your life as a compassionate, purpose-centered and successful entrepreneur? *(The Ordinary World – The Everyday World)*
2	In your elementary through middle school years, what ideas or beliefs were you exposed to that could be a hindrance to your life as a successful, compassionate, purpose-centered entrepreneur? *(The Ordinary World – The Everyday World)*
3	What are the 5 W's of your inner practice? What form of meditation do you practice? When do you meditate? Where do you meditate? With whom do you meditate? Or who are friends or associates who also meditate? Why do you meditate? What benefits have you derived / do you derive? *(Crossing the Threshold – Inner Practice)*
4	What are some early memories and indicators that you were meant to be an entrepreneur, and that you would be involved in your particular purpose? Share some memories of activities that led to your commitment to your purpose as you now define it. Considering the person that you are *now*, what is it about you that makes you well-suited to your purpose? And what are goals in your purposeful life that will require or channel your natural talents, traits, skills, qualities, etc.? *(Embarking on the journey – Commitment to purpose)*

The Hero's Journey Card Values 5 - 8

5	What do you and your customers have in common regarding how you value your product, service, or content? What do you and your customers have in common regarding your interests, your activities, your thoughts, feelings, aspirations, etc.?	
	(Embarking on the journey – Commitment to purpose)	
6	How would you describe an egocentric person? Why is being egocentric a weak position? How can success in one's purposeful life make one egocentric? How can one avoid or stop being egocentric? How does this relate to you and your purpose?	
	(The Abyss – Transcending the ego)	
7	What is the greatest challenge in your achieving success as a compassionate and socially-minded entrepreneur? What is the greatest personal obstacle you must overcome to become the person you intend to be? What must be done to meet the challenges? What are steps *you* will take to meet the challenges?	
	(The Abyss – Transcending the ego)	
8	What insights, revelations, or wisdom have you discovered so far on your journey? What good fortune, unexpected help, higher, inner, deeper guidance, serendipity, windfall, etc. are you grateful for on your journey?	
	(Supernatural Guidance – Inner Guidance)	

The Hero's Journey Card Values 9 - K

9	*Which of the following terms do you prefer related to receiving guidance from another place? Inner (for intuition). Higher (for super- or supranatural), Deeper (for unconscious processes). What are your thoughts and feelings about it/them?* *(Supernatural Guidance – Inner Guidance)*
10	Share how you have grown in your mental, emotional, social, and inner development, and how your growth is supportive to your purpose, mission, and success as an entrepreneur. *(Transformation - The Inner Self)*
J	Share how you want to, or need to, further grow in your mental, emotional, social, and inner development to support your purpose, mission, and success as an entrepreneur. *(Transformation - The Inner Self)*
Q	When you have completely fulfilled your current purpose, what would your life look like? What will you be doing? Where will you be? With whom will you be interacting? How will you change inwardly? *(The New Reality - Inner Life)*
K	What is the gift that you are bringing to the world through your purpose? How will the world be changed as you fulfill your purpose? How will the world be a better place? *(The New Reality – inner Life)*

Key Quotes

NAME

The Hero's Journey mythological structure can be found, in some capacity, in almost every movie we watch. So, here is one last Key Quest game activity, with the name, *Key Quotes* referring to quotes from movies that can be used to support our inner journey as an entrepreneur. Other game options include choosing inspiring *song* quotes or quotes from inspiring societal leaders.

FRAME

The frame of *Key Quotes* is that of a self-selection game, in which a quote is chosen. The play involves selecting your quote, and deriving inspiration, insight, wisdom, etc. from it to support your inner journey as an entrepreneur, either generally or concerning a specific aspect of your journey. So, you begin by presenting your situation or challenge. Then you perform the quote that provides an insight or a solution to the challenge. To add to the game aspect, you can give clues if the person or people involved don't readily know the reference. You can also perform the quote as an actor, singer, speaker, or give your own personal interpretation. Performance can be scored on your personal delivery, and/or how it inspired the other participants, players, or audience.

AIM

The aim of *Key Quotes* is to support your personal, social, entrepreneurial, and inner growth and development. And of course, the game can be played solo, with friends, family members, associates, partners, etc.

Key Quotes Examples

Here are examples of movie and song quotes game play, beginning with a situation, followed by the quote and quote information, and completing with an affirmation.

Situation/Challenge
Sometimes in meditation, I reach a point where I feel no urges, no motivation. It's a calm and powerful feeling. I question how this can be valuable to me, since being motivated is considered a necessary key to success.

Movie Quote
*"My style? You can call it
'The Art of Fighting Without Fighting.'"
(Bruce Lee in 'Enter the Dragon')*

Affirmation
My *habits* that turn into reliable *skills* allow me to calmly and confidently perform 'in the zone', without always needing extrinsic motivations to succeed.

Situation/Challenge
I want to keep a positive mindset regarding others, so that I can stay authentic and true to my purpose and mission of *helping* others ... and feel more genuine joy *for* others.

Song Quote
*"Wishin' you the best, pray that you are blessed.
Much success, no stress, and lots of happiness."
('Survivor' by Destiny's Child)*

Affirmation
When I observe people in the comings and goings of my daily life, I will make a wish for their wellbeing.

Situation/Challenge
On the inner journey of the entrepreneur, it is important to remember that an inner journey means one that leads to ultimate reality, and that finding ultimate reality involves qualities like Peace, Truth, and mainly Love.

Leadership Quote
*"Love is somehow the key
that unlocks the door
which leads to ultimate reality."
(Martin Luther King Jr.)*

Affirmation
Every day I will remind myself of the importance of Love while on my inner journey.

Situation/Challenge
As I am reading, researching, and learning more ideas that support my inner journey as an entrepreneur, I am finding that the more valuable ideas and words I learn, the more relaxed and confident I feel on my journey. I realize that I am learning a new language in a way. The same way that speaking a language helps us to get around in a foreign country, this new language is helping me to get around in our land of opportunity, our land of unlimited possibilities. I'm not sure exactly how this is happening, but it is.

Movie Quote
*"It's the theory that the language you speak
determines how you think."
(Amy Adams in 'Arrival')*

Affirmation
Every day, I add to my knowledge and vocabulary that support my purpose of helping others.

Situation/Challenge
I need to learn how to fulfill orders – how to receive them, create labels, ship them, track them. It's a new and different process for me to learn. It feels hard simply because it is something new and different.

Movie Quote
"It's supposed to be hard. If it wasn't hard, everyone would do it. The hard is what makes it great."
(Tom Hanks in 'A League of their Own')

Affirmation
Regarding (task), I accept the challenge
and embrace the activity that it involves.

Situation/Challenge
Sometimes I overthink things. To handle this challenge, I need to get out of my thinking mind and into action. Sometimes it's about worry. Sometimes it's thinking about perceived mistakes from my past that holds me back. And sometimes it's just not having a needed skill to proceed.

Song Quote
*"Get on your feet. Get up and make it happen.
Get on your feet. Stand up and take some action."*
('Get on your Feet' by Gloria Estefan)

Affirmation
Once I clearly define a goal, I will stop thinking about it, and *take* action. I realize that *mentally* thinking about something can't make it happen in *physical* reality.
So, I will take action, think about the outcome, and then take the next action. By *learning from* my actions, I will ultimately *make it happen* and achieve my goal.

Made in the USA
Middletown, DE
20 September 2022

10364113R00156